IMPACT SHIFT

The Art of Pivoting
for Meaningful Change

DR. RAHUL R. PRASAD

ISBN **979-8-9940696-0-8** (pbk)
ISBN **979-8-9940696-1-5** (hcv)
ISBN **979-8-9940696-2-2** (ebook)

Library of Congress Control Number: **2025926143**

Praise

There are thousands of how-to books, but few of them really matter. This one does.

If you wish to leave the world a better place but don't know how, Prasad's book will guide you. Step by step, he shows you how to create a path that will change your life, the lives of others, and leave a meaningful legacy.

It is a book suffused with joy.
–Jeff Kleeman | CEO, Bold Films; writer of *The Man from U.N.C.L.E.*; producer of *Green Eggs and Ham*; studio executive on *Tomorrow Never Dies* and other films and television series

Impact Shift is worth reading because it shows how real change happens through small, disciplined pivots made over decades, illustrated not just by success stories but by the quiet decisions, doubts, and course corrections most leaders never talk about.
–Dr. Mark N. Harvey | Author of *Single-Minded Leadership*, Harvey Family Foundation

Rahul's work reminds us that a great university is more than a locus of scholarship; it is a living, breathing community sustained by people who believe in giving back. In that sense, Rahul's instrumental leadership as a volunteer and philanthropist has helped ensure that Yale's promise is extended across generations.
– Lynn Cooley | Dean, Graduate School of Arts and Sciences; Vice Provost for Postdoctoral Affairs | Yale University

Table of Contents

Dedication

To my wife, Sharmila Majumdar, who's responsible for the happiest impact shift of my life.

Introduction

"It is every man's obligation to put back into the world at least the equivalent of what he takes out of it."
        —Albert Einstein, *The World as I See It*[1]

I WAS BORN in India in the city of New Delhi, and for the bulk of my childhood, my primary influences came from my grandparents. On my mother's side were Radhakrishna Gupta (Nanaji) and Parvati Gupta (Nani), and on my father's side were Gaya Prasad (Dada) and Ramkali Prasad (Dadi). I was also influenced by my mother's younger sister, Kinni.

That's not to say my parents didn't influence me, but rather that their influence was overshadowed by that of my grandparents, who shaped the child I was and the person I am today. They taught me that you should go out of your way to do things for those who are less fortunate than you.

My grandmothers would never turn a hungry person away from their house. Whenever we had delivery people or workers at the house, my grandmothers would always ask if they wanted something to eat. In those days, beggars would go from house to house, knocking on doors to ask for money. My grandmothers made sure that they were never turned away without food, even if they had no money to give.

For his part, Dada helped to fund and establish a hospital for poor people who had problems with their eyesight. He was very passionate about the project and kept doing it well into his retirement.

---

[1] Albert Einstein, *The World As I See It* (New York: Friede, 1934).

Both of my grandfathers were born and raised back when India was governed by the British. They spent most of their working lives in the civil service, employed by the British Indian government—Dada retiring before the British left India, and Nanaji retiring shortly after Indian independence. In those days, pivoting wasn't much of an option. Once you finished your schooling and got a job, you stayed in that job at that company until you retired, when they gave you a pension and you lived happily ever after. There was no question of moving elsewhere or doing something different.

Dada passed away when I was about sixteen years old, while Nanaji lived much longer because there was a big difference between their ages. Nanaji, in particular, taught me that being kind and honest is what really matters. He taught me to have integrity, to stick to my ideals, and to follow my conscience, regardless of whether that came at a cost.

When I was a teenager, Nanaji told me that he could have continued in the civil service for longer but that he chose not to because he'd been asked to countersign a report that he believed was wrong. He wasn't willing to lend the weight of his office to a faulty report because he was an engineer and he worried that if the construction went ahead, there'd be an accident that could result in property damage or even death. He didn't want that to happen and so he chose to step aside, despite the fact that it came at a personal cost.

That taught me early on that if things aren't going in the way that you want them to go, it's a good idea to pivot and to do something different. That's where it all started.

Giving Back at Yale

Dada was a firm believer in education, so he made sure that my father and I were privately educated. I was never part of the elite, but we were relatively well-to-do, and I never lacked for anything. I was certainly privileged, and the path ahead of me was smoothed.

All of my peers came from well-educated, well-heeled families, but they didn't place much emphasis on giving back to the community. It wasn't a big part of the culture, or at least, not in the time and place where I grew up.

The idea of being charitable—of doing things for other people—was at the back of my mind, but it didn't truly come to the forefront until I came to the US in 1982. I'd completed an undergraduate degree in physics and wanted to pursue postgraduate education in the US so that I could earn a PhD.

In India, you study a bachelor's degree for three years, while in the United States, you usually study for four. When I applied to study my PhD in the US, most of the colleges wanted me to have studied for four years and so they only offered me an admission to a bachelor's degree program. Yale was different. They said they couldn't tell whether I was ready to take on a graduate degree, but they asked me to send my coursework so they could take a look.

They looked at me as a person and not as a number, and so when they offered me a place, I knew that I had to take it because they saw me for who I really was. I've never felt more at home in any place than I did when I was at Yale.

Yale has a Center for Public Service and Social Justice called Dwight Hall, founded in 1858. It is home to over 60 undergraduate-run community service groups.[2] It's an integral part of campus where both undergraduate and graduate students can sign up to help out in the community.

I visited Dwight Hall and participated in a few activities, although not as many as I would have liked. I was busy trying to do my research work and to finish my thesis, and it was a race against time. Three years in, my thesis advisor decided to quit, and I had enough funding to either finish up in one year or to start over from

---

[2] "Service," *Yale University*, accessed October 9, 2025, https://www.yale.edu/life-yale/service.

scratch. That left me working around the clock during my fourth year of graduate school so that I didn't have to start all over again.

Still, Dwight Hall taught me that giving back and being part of a community was extremely important.

Cleaning up the Bay

At the time, when I moved to New Haven, there weren't many foreign students at Yale and so they paired every foreign student with a host family. The foreign students usually couldn't go back to their home countries for holidays like Thanksgiving and Christmas, and it's lonely to be on a campus when everyone else has left. By pairing them up with the local families, Yale made sure we always had somewhere to go.

My host parents, Ellen and Walter Griest, had both spent some time in India in the Peace Corps–and they were yet another example of people who went out of their way to do something for others. We're talking about two well-off folks from the US, the son and daughter of farmers and engineers on both sides of the family, living comfortably in Connecticut. And yet after they finished college, they spent several years working in villages in rural India. How much less selfish can you be?

Meanwhile, a lot of my mentors were on the faculty, and most of them were carving out some time alongside their daily work and their family commitments to work in the community. They provided me with some further reminders that it's important to make the world a better place, whether you're volunteering at the local food bank or spending years of your life serving the poor and underprivileged in India.

By the time I graduated, I was married. My wife and I met as undergraduates in India, and we decided that we loved California so much that we wanted to live there. Shortly after arriving in the Golden State, we both started working and we soon had our first child. I got wrapped up in having a career and raising a family, and so the idea of service and helping others started to fall by the wayside, but it was always there at the back of my mind.

When we first moved here in the late 80s, there was a lot of pollution in San Francisco Bay. Junk used to float away from the garbage dumps on the edge of the bay and end up on the beaches, so every once in a while, the community would organize a beach cleanup. We'd participate in those, spending the best part of the morning picking up trash, getting to know our neighbors and the community, and doing our bit to help clean up.

But there was something missing, and as we'll discuss in the coming chapters, it took my children to show me what that was.

The First Man on the Moon

I got interested in being a scientist as a kid back in July 1969, after I watched Neil Armstrong set foot on the moon. I couldn't believe what I was seeing and so I turned to my dad and asked, "What did Neil Armstrong do to become the first man on the moon?" He told me, "Well, he's a scientist."

As it turned out, that's not exactly right because Neil Armstrong was a test pilot, not a scientist. Still, Armstrong is the reason why I got into the field, starting out with pure science before moving to applied physics and then to mechanical engineering.

Later on, I was given the chance to join a company working on plasma physics and electrical discharges, as opposed to staying in academia or working on mechanical engineering. It also gave my wife and me a chance to move to San Francisco, as she'd been offered a job at the University of California. We were moving to California.

Several pivots later, which I won't go into here, I started working at the Lawrence Livermore National Lab. It was super exciting because it meant switching careers once again: from working with plasma physics and electrical discharges to working with lasers. More specifically, my job was to work on the glass that's used to focus them.

The National Ignition Facility, which housed the nuclear fusion projects of the United States for a number of years, had a problem where the glass would start to get damaged because of how high the laser intensity was. My group ended up developing a way in which we could toughen the glass, as well as to fix the damage when it occurred, and that helped us to create a laser that's powerful enough to generate fusion.

Over the next few decades, the researched advanced to the point where we achieved breakeven, when the energy that's coupled into the reaction is less than the amount of energy that comes out of it. That's the first step towards making a practical nuclear fusion reactor, which we hope will one day become a reality.

Most people would be happy working on a project like that, but I'd started volunteering for Yale–going back to the campus and talking with the students. I realized that I enjoyed volunteering and helping people to find their passion much more than I enjoyed working on nuclear fusion.

The laser was invented over 60 years ago, and it didn't take long for nuclear fusion to be considered as a real possibility.[3] Fast forward to today, and we're still several decades away from a nuclear fusion power plant from being a practical reality. It's one of those fields where it takes years for any significant change to take place, and that just wasn't for me anymore.

During that time, I'd also started getting more involved with the alumni association. I started out with the Graduate School Alumni

---

[3] Hank Hogan and Melinda Rose, "A History of the Laser: 1960 - 2019," *Photonics Media*, March 5, 2024, https://www.photonics.com/Articles/A_History_of_the_Laser_1960_-_2019/a42279

Association at Yale and progressed through the ranks, becoming an officer and eventually chairing the association, after which I decided to join the broader alumni association for the entire university. Yet again, I rose to executive officer and then became chair.

That was a first in a number of different ways. I was the first person with a graduate school degree to lead the alumni association in its history. I was also the first person of Indian American origin. I was a trailblazer in a lot of ways, and I'm proud of having done that. It's also what showed me that public service was more attractive to me than my work as a scientist.

That brings me to 2018, when I chose to seek early retirement, although I continued to consult in my field for a while. That allowed me to hold on to the apron strings for a while and to have a safety blanket instead of letting go completely as I jumped into the deep blue sea of public service.

I started working more closely with Butterflies USA, joining the board and eventually becoming president. It was also at that time that I met Scott Clark, another Yale alumnus, in San Francisco, which is what led to my involvement with Amandla.

But I'm getting ahead of myself, and that's a story for later on. In the meantime, I hope that this gives you a good idea of who I am, where I come from, and what I'm all about. And now that our introductions are out of the way, we can begin.

It's time for us to sow the seeds of change.

PART ONE

Seeds of Change

CHAPTER ONE

The Butterfly Effect

"Ask not what your country can do for you—ask what you can do for your country."

—John F. Kennedy[4]

WHEN MY KIDS were in elementary school, we were living in Alameda, and the local schools weren't the best, so we sent them to the local Catholic school. Part of that was because my wife had gone to Catholic schools growing up and so she was attuned to the culture. Neither of us was Catholic, but we both thought it was the right decision.

Of course, Catholics and Catholic schools are big on the idea of charity and doing work within the community, and so our kids soon started getting involved with all that. It brought me full circle, and it's interesting how my grandparents and my kids both taught me the same thing—that it's important to give back to the community as much as you can.

And so we started raising funds for the school and taking part in their various community initiatives that were aimed at helping local children who were less fortunate. That became an important part of our lives.

When John F. Kennedy delivered his famous inauguration speech, the one that includes the line that kicks off this chapter, he was focusing specifically on his country, the United States. It's a fantastic quote, but what makes it most interesting here is its flexibility.

---

[4] Nathan Rott, "'Ask Not . . .': JFK's words still inspire 50 years later," *NPR*, January 18, 2011, https://www.npr.org/2011/01/18/133018777/jfks-inaugural-speech-still-inspires-50-years-later

You can scale it up and say, "Ask not what the world can do for you–ask what you can do for the world." Or you can narrow it down to, "Ask not what people can do for you–ask what you can do for people."

That makes his quote the linguistic equivalent of a fractal, in that it looks the same regardless of the scale at which you look at it. Other fractals include rivers, snowflakes, tree branches, and copper crystals.[5]

Going back to Kennedy, it's his idea of asking what you can do for the world which led to my family and I volunteering in the local community (and beyond).

I also wanted to include Kennedy because he was largely responsible for the United States putting the first man on the moon, although he didn't live to see it, and I've already mentioned how that was a seminal moment in my own life. In 1962, Kennedy gave a speech at Rice Stadium which aimed to persuade the American public to support the Apollo program in which he said, "We choose to go to the moon in this decade and do the other things not because they are easy, but because they are hard. Because that goal will serve to organize and measure the best of our energies and skills, because that challenge is one that we're willing to accept. One we are unwilling to postpone."[6]

He could just as easily have been talking about donating our time and money so that we can help those who are less fortunate than us.

When my daughter was in middle school and my son was in elementary school, we took a trip to visit our parents (and the kids' grandparents) in India. When school's out during the summer, it's too hot, and so it makes a lot more sense to go during winter.

---

[5] Shea Gunther, "9 amazing fractals found in nature," *Treehugger*, May 30, 2024, https://www.treehugger.com/amazing-fractals-found-in-nature-4868776

[6] John F. Kennedy (JFK) Moon Speech Transcript: "We Choose To Go To the Moon," *Rev,* n.d., https://www.rev.com/transcripts/john-f-kennedy-jfk-moon-speech-transcript-we-choose-to-go-to-themoon

We decided to visit in February, which is the best time to go because it's neither too hot nor too cold, but school was still in session and so we had to ask if it was okay for the kids to take a couple of weeks off. They told us that was fine, as long as they did their homework.

At the time, my daughter was working on a class project where she had to put in a certain number of hours of community service. We wanted to know if she could do that in India and they said, "Absolutely, as long as she has some proof to show that she did the project."

I didn't know of any organizations in India that she might be able to get involved with, but I thought of a family friend named Kathy Gerardi who used to participate in a program called Butterflies in New Delhi. I called and told her I was going to India and asked if she could put us in touch with the folks at Butterflies.

Butterflies

Butterflies is a registered voluntary organization that has been working with the most vulnerable groups of children–street children in particular–since its creation in 1989. As they explain on their website, "The organization endeavors to educate and impart life skills to vulnerable children so that they become self-reliant and exit the generational cycle of illiteracy and poverty. Butterflies also has a research, liaising and training wing that works to support mobilization of civil society and influences policies at all levels."[7]

The organization's name comes from the idea that childhood, like a butterfly, only lasts for a short time and is beautiful. And just like a caterpillar turns into a butterfly, children, too, undergo a metamorphosis as they grow into adults. Butterflies aims to help marginalized kids–those who don't have the kind of advantages

---

[7] "About Us," Butterflies NGO, last modified August 14, 2024, https://butterfliesngo.org/about-us.

you get with a good home and well-off parents—to spread their wings and fly.

Butterflies was founded in India by an amazing woman called Rita Panicker. It's headquartered in New Delhi, but the Butterflies model has grown wings (if you'll pardon the pun) and has been adopted elsewhere in India, often with government support.

Kathy put me in touch with Rita, and so I called her up and offered to help. She said, "That would be great! We have contact centers where we house children who've either run away or who've been separated and who got lost from their families. We house them there while we try to find their parents and see whether it's appropriate to reunite them with their families, because it's not always a good idea. We don't want to reunite them if they've run away because they were being abused, but if it was an accidental separation then that's a different story."

It's surprisingly easy for kids to get lost in India—after all, it is a country of over 1.4 billion people, with dozens of sprawling cities each home to millions. When kids get lost, it's difficult to reunite them with their parents because it's like looking for a biological needle in a haystack. When young children are separated from their families, you can ask them who their parents are and where they come from, but they'll say that their mom is "Mom," their dad is "Dad," and that they live "at home." When that's all you know about someone, it's not easy to find out who their parents are.

There's a shortage of supplies in the places where these kids are living, which causes problems because we want to entertain them and give them an education while we wait to reunite them with their families. Rita told me that they were in particular need of art supplies, and so our kids went around the neighborhood and the local schools and collected three suitcases full of art supplies for us to bring along.

The plan was to deliver the supplies to Butterflies and then to go on with our vacation, but our children decided they wanted to stay. They didn't speak the same language as the Indian kids, yet they still managed to communicate in the way that kids do.

We were in Delhi for four days, and we visited the Butterflies contact center every day. We tried to convince our kids to go and see all of city's sights and monuments that are popular among tourists, but they didn't want to go because that would mean that they wouldn't get to spend as much time with the kids at Butterflies.

The Khazana

When I visited the contact center in India during a later visit, I was struck by the joy and enthusiasm I saw in the faces of the social workers that were helping the children, and even more so in the faces of the children themselves.

The goal of the contact center is to provide a safe space where children living in the neighborhood, typically out on the streets, can come to congregate with one another, as well as with the social workers. During my first visit, when they introduced me as a visitor from America, I sensed some hesitance from the kids. Fortunately, because of my own background, I was able to ask them a question in their language, which broke the ice. One of the kids raised his hand and started speaking, and then the floodgates opened.

Before I knew it, they were telling me all about the Khazana, a word which means *treasury* in Hindi. The Khazana came about because Butterflies tried to open a cooperative bank for the children but were turned down by the banks because they weren't licensed to do so. They didn't have the right certifications and so they couldn't use the word "bank." Butterflies said, "Okay, we'll call it a treasury." Apparently, that was acceptable.

I asked the kids how the Khazana works, and they told me that there were eight or ten of them who ran the Khazana for a year.

They're taught how to create accounts, and how to add credits and debits to those accounts. They take the cash, they count it, and at the end of the day, all of the cash is given to one of the social workers. The social worker takes it and deposits it into the Butterflies bank account so that it can earn interest, and then that interest is given back to the children.

The Khazana also helps the kids to get into the habit of spending their money wisely and saving for the future. If one of the kids who made a deposit wants to withdraw some of their money, they have to say what they're going to use it for. Then the group of kids who've been chosen to head the bank decide whether it's a good use of money or not.

When I asked how they decide whether it's a good use of money or not, they told me that they perform an undercover operation. If one of the kids says that they need the money because their relative is sick and they need to buy medicine, they'll send a couple of people to the neighborhood to find out whether their relative is really sick or whether it's just a ruse to get hold of the cash.

I was worried about favoritism, and so I wanted to know what was to stop them from granting withdrawals for their friends and not to anyone else. They had a solution for that, too.

"We have a general meeting once a month where we all get together," the kids explained. "If we want to, we can vote the people on the board out. If two-thirds of the people say they want to vote the leaders out, then the leaders get voted out, and we start again."

If you're interested in politics, then you might recognize that as a recall election. I was fascinated by this, because it meant that as aside from learning about finance, the children were also learning about governance and society as a whole.

The Power of Cooperation

As the Khazana shows, Butterflies is all about helping children to prepare for their future, and it's this that convinced me to raise money for the program.

For example, they have a program called the Butterflies School for Culinary and Catering (BSCC), where older kids (generally 17- and 18-year-olds) can train as apprentices and learn to be professional chefs. As part of the BSCC, Butterflies has partnered with several five-star hotels and a number of high-end restaurants.

The hotels and restaurants take the kids we've trained and give them apprenticeships, which later turn into permanent jobs if all goes well. Some of the kids decide to become entrepreneurs instead, and so we help them to fund and finance a food cart. In India, there are plenty of street corners where there's a ton of pedestrian traffic, and so they can set up shop and start making money by themselves instead of working for a restaurant.

Several years after I started working with Butterflies, I was taking a look at a video they'd shot in India for us to use while fundraising in the US. I watched as they interviewed one of the teachers, who turned out to be a former student who said that his life had been so transformed by Butterflies that he wanted to give back and to help the next generation of children to experience the same kind of transformation.

Butterflies is also known for cooperative learning, where the children learn together and teach one another. The goal is to supplement what they're being taught in school by providing a place where they can go to do their homework in a supportive environment. It provides them with a much-needed space where they can focus on their work without their parents saying, "Stop doing your homework and go out to earn some money."

Uneducated parents often don't see the value of an education, viewing it as a waste of time. To them, a fifteen-year-old kid could be lifting boxes somewhere for a few bucks a day instead of burying his nose in a book. They're so worried about putting food on the table that they don't think of education as something that could give their child a better life in the future.

Butterflies helps to change that, allowing the kids to get together with a social worker and to concentrate on their studies. The older kids are often able to help the younger ones, and that seems to stick better. It also means that when they ask an adult for help or when they go back to school for their regular lessons, they're doing so because they want to learn.

Joining the Board

After our trip to Delhi, I kept in touch with the team and donated little sums of money whenever I could, but I still wanted to do more. Helping children has always been close to my heart, in part because of the old (but true) cliché that children are our future.

By that point, my friend Joe, Kathy Gerardi's son, had become a member of the board of Butterflies USA, which is dedicated to raising funds for Butterflies in India. He told me that they were doing a campaign, and he was working on a video for it, but he was struggling with the translations. There were times when there was a minute's worth of conversation and he'd been given three or four words as the translation, so he had a feeling that they weren't accurate.

Sure enough, we started going through it and I found that the translator had taken some real liberties and done a shoddy job. I started providing the translations, and as we were talking, he asked me if I'd mind narrating the video. He said that they hadn't settled on a voiceover artist and that he liked the sound of my voice and the authenticity I could bring. I have enough of an accent that people can tell I'm from India, but my diction is clear enough that people can understand what I'm saying, even if they speak English as a second language. They weren't going to have to subtitle me, like they had to do for the people in New Delhi.

I agreed and narrated the video for him, and the rest is history. I've been doing it ever since.

During my second year with Butterflies, my friend told me that they had a board opening and asked if I'd like to join. Before I knew it, I was sitting on the board, helping them to define how they raise money. We went from making a few thousand dollars a year from little events like yoga classes to running campaigns aimed at getting high net worth individuals to make larger contributions. The goal was to have fewer people giving money but for them to be writing bigger checks so that we could more easily reach our objectives.

Of course, that's not to say that grassroots efforts don't have a place, because even the smallest donation helps. On top of that, you never know when you might find someone who gives $25 the first time but then gets super interested and gives you $2,500 tomorrow. You've got to reach out in every direction.

The Art of Saying Yes

I must have done something right to impress the board because when the president retired, she asked if I'd take over her role. It goes to show how saying yes to one thing at a time can all add up and lead to something bigger.

But there's another part to this equation, which is that if you don't take chances and try new things, you're stuck. You only know what you know, and nobody can claim that they know everything. If you want to make changes in your life then the only way to get from point A to point B is to take chances, and that requires you to ask the question, "Why not?"

Sometimes, there's a solid answer to that. You might ask yourself that question and say, "This isn't the right thing to do. It's dangerous, deleterious, or against my conscience." When that's the case, it's fine to say no and move on. You don't have to go down every path and say yes to everything, but at the same time, it's always a good idea to dip your toes into uncharted territory. It keeps you fresh, it keeps you young, and it keeps you thinking.

As one of my mentors told me many years ago: "The day you stop learning is the day you discover you're six feet under."

> ▷ **Action Item:** Say yes to something that you'd normally say no to–something outside of your comfort zone. Better yet, commit to saying yes to things that you'd normally say no to for the next week. Monitor the effects it has on your life and whether you learn anything new about yourself.

CHAPTER TWO

Shaping a Philanthropic Vision

"When I come home to you, San Francisco, your golden sun will shine for me."

–Tony Bennett, "I Left My Heart in San Francisco"

GETTING INVOLVED WITH BUTTERFLIES got me thinking that giving back was a good idea, but other than a few small projects in our local community, the next opportunity didn't present itself until 2001, when I picked up an email from Yale, asking if I'd be interested in volunteering at the alumni association.

I said yes without thinking too much about it; I just filled out the questionnaire they'd sent out and then forgot all about it.

Nothing happened for a year or so, but then in early 2002, I got a call from an unknown number. I picked it up and found myself talking to a gentleman called Steve Scher, who was the chair of the Graduate School Alumni Association (GSAA).

Steve told me that one of their board members had been unable to complete his three-year term and was stepping aside with two years still remaining. They wanted to know if I'd be interested in filling his shoes, which would mean going back to New Haven twice a year for GSAA meetings. These gatherings brought alumni delegates and leaders of the alumni community from around the globe come together to talk about what's going on at the university, what it needs and how the alumni can help.

The GSAA only needed me to go to four meetings to complete the term. I hadn't been back since leaving in 1989, and so I thought it would be a wonderful thing to do and an easy commitment to make. I was already planning trips to see the Griests and thinking about catching up with my old acquaintances.

It turned out that the board consisted of a couple dozen alumni from various departments of the graduate school. I wasn't just talking to other scientists; there were art historians, social scientists, and all sorts of other people, and everyone had different ideas and different visions of the future.

During that very first meeting, I was struck by how strange it was that people were spending most of their time talking about the problems they'd faced when they were graduate students, which ranged from a couple of years to three, four, or even five decades earlier. It didn't seem like a productive use of our time. If we couldn't talk about how we'd make things better in the future, then what was the point of us being there? Sitting around and complaining about the past wasn't helping anyone.

Playing Our Part

By the time that I went back for my second meeting in April 2003, I'd spent some time thinking how we could be more effective. When we sat down and started the meeting, I said, "We've spent a lot of time talking about how things were. May I suggest that we talk about how things could be if we played our part?"

There was a stunned silence around the room, but they humored me.

We had reunions for the graduate school, but they were all based around particular fields. You'd get people who graduated with a degree in engineering all coming back at the same time and talking to each other.

"That's fine," I explained, "and I'm not suggesting that it's a bad idea, but I also think it would be useful to have alumni coming back in cohorts based upon the year."

In other words, if you graduated in 1989, you should be able to attend a reunion for people who graduated between 1986 and 1992. It would bring people together who were on campus at the same time but who aren't necessarily in the same field. They wouldn't be strangers, though—they'd be people you met through extra-curricular activities, the friends you were likely closer to than your classmates.

The other members of the GSAA thought it was a good idea, but it would mean going from being a passive organization to being an active one.

Fast forward to April 2004, when I finished my term after two more meetings and several positive discussions about how we could more fruitfully engage with the faculty and students. I thought my time with the GSAA was over, because there was a rule that you could only serve a single term. It made sense, because they wanted new people to come in and be leaders so that they didn't end up stuck with the same old faces.

But there was a loophole. Steve told me that because I'd only served a partial term after taking over from someone else, I could still run to be elected. That's how I ended serving a three-year term of my own, and that's also how my ideas about bringing people together from different fields began to materialize.

Where Do I Go from Yale?

My concept continued to grow and evolve, turning into an inter-disciplinary workshop that would focus on some need that covered multiple disciplines. For example, one of the ideas was to talk about the US healthcare system and how it could be improved. That would be of interest to everyone, regardless of whether or not they were in the healthcare field, because everyone interacts with the healthcare system.

Then the 2008 financial crisis hit, the largest and most severe financial event since the Great Depression.[8] Yale had to make a ton of cutbacks, and so the university that had been encouraging us to be ambitious had a sudden shrinking of budgets and told us to put the workshop on the back burner. That left us trying to figure out whether we could go ahead with the workshop without asking Yale for any money.

I'd also completed my three-year term, but it seemed that the leadership team was happy with my work because they asked me to stay on for another year as secretary. I went on to become treasurer, vice chair, and eventually chair in 2010.

Around the same time as I became chair of the GSAA, the graduate school got a new dean. His name was Tom Pollard, and he held an MD as opposed to a PhD. He'd been leading the search for a new dean, but they'd been unable to find anyone, and so the committee offered him the position instead because he had some great ideas about what the graduate school should be like.

I went straight over to see him on a trip that I paid for out of my own pocket, and the two of us realized that we had a lot in common. I explained that a lot of our PhD students were trying to get academic jobs, but that there weren't many of them left and that the number of them was dropping every day.

"Luckily," I said, "I've got an idea. Why don't we host a conference where we bring alumni back to campus to talk about the careers that have taken them outside of academics?"

"Let's do it," Tom replied.

We decided to run a pilot where we'd bring in alumni who were already coming to campus as part of the GSAA. We also

---

[8] Wall Street Oasis, "Financial Banking Crisis 2008 - Detailed Overview," accessed October 9, 2025, https://www.wallstreetoasis.com/financial-banking-crisis-2008-overview

approached a few others who were close enough to New Haven that they could drive, and so we wouldn't need to pay for flights and hotels. Yale said we could use their classrooms, and so as long as we could find a little money to buy some food and cover gas money, we figured we could make it happen.

We put the pilot together and called it Where Do I Go from Yale?– and it was a rip-roaring success. The students loved it, and so did the alumni. There's nothing more refreshing for a person that's been away from the campus for a few years to come back and to talk to young people. It rejuvenates you and gives you a ton of new ideas. It makes you feel alive again.

Fifteen years have passed since that first event, and I'm pleased to be able to say that at the time of writing, I was getting ready to travel back to Yale to celebrate its anniversary.

Yes, But Where Did *I* Go from Yale?

When I graduated from Yale, I didn't have anyone to help me to find a job. To compound that struggle even further, my wife graduated at the same time as me and she was looking for work, too.

We were both engineers, albeit with different specializations, and we were determined to find work in the same city, because we'd seen other couples who'd graduated before us going to live in different cities and having difficult lives. As well as struggling to set up their careers, they were fighting to keep their relationships going with hundreds or thousands of miles between them. This was in the late 80s, when there was no such thing as video calls or social networking. We had letters and phone calls, and phone calls didn't come cheap. We didn't want to do that.

As it happened, the first job I got after graduating happened to be at Yale itself, and my wife got an offer to work there as an assistant professor. We decided to stay for a while, but we'd visited California in 1985 and left our hearts in San Francisco, and so we knew that as soon as one of us got an opportunity to work in California, we'd move there.

I got a job offer in the Bay Area in 1988, and so my wife and I decided to go for it. It took us about a year to wrap everything up at Yale, but my future employer was very patient and told me to take my time because they really wanted me to join them.

We moved to California in July 1989, where I started by working at a large company before joining a small business and then becoming an entrepreneur. I tried to buy the small business with a couple of my colleagues, but that didn't fly because you can't buy what isn't for sale, and so we decided to set up our own company instead.

I stayed with that company for about eight years, but my cofounders and I didn't see eye-to-eye on the fundamental issue of what the company should become when it grew bigger. I'd been reading books about entrepreneurship and wanted it to be a commercial venture, but the others were more risk-averse. I learned a lot of things from that company, but perhaps the most important lesson was that if you go into business with other people, you need to have a commonality of purpose, otherwise it's never going to work.

And so we parted ways, which led to me joining the Lawrence Livermore National Laboratory in around 2002. That was when Steve called me up and asked me to join the GSAA.

Luckily, my then-boss Dick Hackel gave me plenty of encouragement. He pointed out that if I went back to New Haven and met up with students from the graduate school, I might be able to recruit the next generation of scientists and engineers. He told me to take as much time as I needed and not to bother charging it to my vacation time. If any of the students I spoke to came in for an interview, they'd cover the cost of my trip as a business expense.

That made going out a whole lot easier.

A Personal Discovery

The Where Do I Go from Yale? program taught me an important lesson. I learned that what really motivates me is to make sure that if I ever go through a situation I'm unhappy with, I do everything within my power to make sure that others don't suffer the same fate. I felt that if I could help students not to suffer from the same loneliness and angst around finding employment that I'd had to deal with, I'd be making the world a better place.

In the second or third installment of the program, a young lady called Dragana Savic came up to me and said, "I know you're not in the medical field, but as this is a networking session, I thought I'd introduce myself. I'm doing a master's degree at Yale, focusing my research on PET-MRIs, and I'm due to graduate in six months. I'm looking for a job, but I don't really know what I'm doing. I was wondering whether you could take a look at my resume and help me to make it more attractive to potential employers. I've never looked for a job before, and I was hoping you'd give me some pointers on how to go about it."

I said yes, of course. It was a cause that was dear to my heart because no one had helped me when I'd been in her shoes. I would have loved to have been given the opportunity that she had, and I was determined to do everything I could to help her.

And so I got hold of her resume and helped her to refine it, but what she didn't know was that I had an ulterior motive. My wife worked with MRIs and had just received a new PET-MRI machine, and she needed someone who knew about PET-MRIs to launch a research program.

I helped her to polish her resume and then showed it to my wife, who said, "Good lord, I'd love to meet her." To cut the long story short, my wife offered her a job, and she moved to California when she graduated. She stayed for a while, discovered that she loved academics and chose to go back to Oxford, where she was admitted to their PhD program. She obtained that, as I knew she would, and is now an entrepreneur who splits her time between London and Boston.

Recently, I was talking to another mentee of mine who's started a business using AI. She had some doubts about what she was doing and was worried that she'd never be successful, but it turned out that she was defining success based upon the amount of money she was earning. I said, "You've got to stop thinking about success as being the pot of gold at the end of the rainbow. Instead, think of success in terms of every step you take along the way. You started out with an idea, and you've already developed a product that people are willing to pay for. To me, that's already an amazing amount of success, and you're not done yet."

She ended the call by saying that she was super glad that we'd connected again because it was the first time in months that she'd felt like she was doing something useful. She was too busy getting caught up in the fact that she hadn't made a million bucks in revenue to realize that in most people's eyes, she was already a success.

The Two Sides of Philanthropy

Whenever I returned to Yale, I went out of my way to talk to as many of the students as I could. I gave out my business card to as many people as I could and told them that if they ever needed advice—or even just someone to listen to them or a friendly voice to bounce ideas off—then they should feel free to give me a shout.

I'd always tell the students that by virtue of finishing a PhD, they will have solved a problem that no one else has solved before. In other words, they're doing original work, and if you can do original work once, you can do it again. When they walked into the PhD program, they knew nothing about the field that they're about to graduate as an expert in. So why be afraid when it comes to getting a job?

Take a job in a field that you know nothing about. You learned a new field five years ago, so you can do it again.

There are two main types of philanthropy. We're all aware of the monetary kind of philanthropy, where those of us who are fortunate enough give money to a good cause. But we can also be #philanthropic by giving people our time and expertise. Time and talent are just as important as treasure, and it allows those of us who aren't so fortunate to make a real difference in the world.

That's why I encourage people to look for ways in which they can give back to their community and to help those who need it, even if that's by doing something small.

There's a wonderful program called Big Brothers Big Sisters of America in which they facilitate mentorships between an older person and a younger person, typically in schools. They explain, "Since 1904, Big Brothers Big Sisters has operated under the belief that inherent in every child is incredible potential. As the nation's largest donor and volunteer supported mentoring network, Big Brothers Big Sisters makes meaningful, monitored matches between adult volunteers ("Bigs") and children ("Littles), ages five through young adulthood in communities across the country."[9]

Programs like this are a great way in which you can help people who are struggling and trying to figure out the ropes. It's the cornerstone of civilized society because we need each other as a species. The only reason why we're where we are today is because we've helped one another along. Yes, we've also done a lot to hurt each other with all of the wars we've fought, but there's light in even the darkest of times. Even during wars, there are stories of incredible bravery and stupendous sacrifices as people risk everything to help one another.

---

[9] "About Us," Big Brothers Big Sisters of America, accessed October 9, 2025, https://www.bbbs.org/about-us.

The San Francisco Symphony

By the time that I started volunteering with the GSAA, my wife and I were giving money to the San Francisco Symphony, an incredible orchestra with over 110 years of history and 17 Grammy award wins to its name.[10] We both love classical music, and we became season subscribers shortly after moving to California in 1989. We were going to see them on a regular basis.

As an engineer, I can't stop making engineering estimates in my daily life. One day, as I was sitting in the Louise M. Davies Symphony Hall, I looked around and figured out that there were around 2,500 seats. I made a mental calculation based on the average ticket price and worked out how much money they made per concert, and then I multiplied that by the number of concerts in a year to determine how much revenue they were bringing in. I took that figure and divided it up amongst the 100+ members of the orchestra and quickly discovered that it didn't add up. They weren't making enough money to live on.

Bear in mind that this only covered the cost of the musicians; I had no way of estimating how much the building cost. It almost didn't matter, because I already knew that if we as the audience members didn't do our fair share by giving what we could in addition to what we'd paid for the tickets, the orchestra wouldn't be around for future generations to enjoy. And so we started giving what little we could.

Now, you might be wondering why I give money to an orchestra when there are so many other fantastic causes out there. The truth is that you can care about multiple issues at once, and you can contribute in different ways. You can give your time, or you can give your money. It might not surprise you to know that it's the latter of the two that's generally the easier option.

---

[10] San Francisco Symphony, "SF Symphony Wins 2025 Grammy Award for Best Opera Recording," February 2, 2025, *San Francisco Press Room*, https://www.sfsymphony.org/About-SFS/Press-Room/Press-Releases/SF-Symphony-wins-2025-Grammy-Award-for-Best-Opera

For example, I'm passionate about animals and so I help them through the coffee I drink. There's a roastery called Muddy Waters Coffee Company, which has a product line called Rescue Roasts—a collection of coffees that gives a percentage of its sales to animal shelters, and so I buy my coffee from there.[11] The coffee costs me a little more than I'd pay at the local supermarket, but I feel better about doing it.

Not everyone can afford to buy fancy coffee. You can give back in whichever way works for you, but most of us have the ability to donate some time. It doesn't have to be a lot and it doesn't have to be structured, but everything you do will make a difference.

Let's say you're walking along the street and you notice some litter. Stop for a second, pick it up, and put it in a trash can. If you're walking down the street, turn to the next person that you come across and smile and say, "Good morning." Politeness doesn't cost anything, and you'll brighten their day.

A lot of people look up to Apple co-founder Steve Jobs, and despite his well-documented flaws, they have good reason to. I look up to Jobs too, but not because of his work at Apple or even his philanthropy. I look up to him because of a simple but profound statement that he made: he said that he wanted to leave the world a better place than he found it.

You can do this in many ways. Jobs did it through his inventions, which made people's lives easier. I do it through my philanthropic work. You can do it by helping someone to cross the street or picking up litter. It's less about what you do and more about the mindset it takes to be on the lookout for these kinds of opportunities. If you adopt Jobs' philosophy as a mantra, you'll start to see these opportunities everywhere you look.

---

[11] For more information about Rescue Roasts, visit https://www.ilovemud.com/collections/rescue-roasts.

PART TWO

The Power of Education

CHAPTER THREE

Stories from Mentoring

"Tell me and I forget. Teach me and I may remember. Involve me and I learn."
                —A quote incorrectly attributed to Benjamin Franklin[12]

WHERE DO I GO FROM YALE? continued to grow each year, and it soon became clear that the most important element of the program was the open networking session. That was where we'd have all of the attendees–both students and alumni–available for discussions, riffing off one another, and expanding upon the discussions that had happened during the formal sessions while simultaneously being open to completely new subject matters.

We started trying to match students and mentors whose interests aligned, knowing that they could have quick conversations with one another before deciding whether they had enough in common to keep talking in the future. We'd pick a cohort of 100 students who wanted mentors and reach out to the alumni body to ask for people who were interested in mentoring. Then we'd use a simple set of questions to gauge interest areas and expertise and start to hand-match students and mentors. This was long before AI algorithms and fancy software packages, so it was a long and labor-intensive process. But it was also incredibly effective.

This side of things was almost like a dating agency–which is ironic, because we later launched a speed mentoring session with a timekeeper at the head of the room, ringing a bell every minute and a half. When the bell sounded, the students had to get up and

---

[12] quoteresearch, "Quote Origin: Tell Me and I Forget; Teach Me and I May Remember; Involve Me and I Learn," February 27, 2019, *Quote Investigator*, https://quoteinvestigator.com/2019/02/27/tell/

move to the mentor at the next table. At the end of the session, we'd collate everyone's responses and match the mentors and students who'd both indicated that they wanted to spend more time together.

It was at one of these sessions that I got my first glimpse of how much a mentor can learn from a mentee, which is the theme of this chapter.

I'd matched with a student, and we ended up having a long conversation that ended with him telling me that he had a unique problem. He knew what career he wanted to get into after he graduated, but he hadn't been sure how he'd keep his connection with Yale going. He told me that I'd taught him a valuable lesson because I'd travelled all the way from California to Connecticut to meet with people and to share what I'd learned about the world–the knowledge I'd gained, the wisdom I'd acquired, and the experiences I'd had.

He decided there and then that he wanted to do that too, and that would be how he'd maintain his connection with Yale.

And that taught me the real power of what I was doing. I was showing people the way forward.

Mentors versus Sponsors

Some people get confused about what a mentor is and so let's take a moment or two to clarify the difference between mentors and sponsors.

A mentor is someone who advocates for you when you're in the room, in the sense that they push you to be your best. They ask you questions, give you advice, and have your best interests at heart. But they only do that when you're in the room with them.

That makes them very different to a sponsor, which is a person who advocates for you even when you're not in the room. They'll speak up on your behalf in promotions meetings and sing your praises to senior management.

I often hear people accusing their mentors of not doing enough for them and not advocating on their behalf, but that's not the mentor's job. The role of a mentor is to help you to be the best you can be. A sponsor will help you to get a promotion or a pay raise, but only if there's something in it for them. If you want someone to be your sponsor then you'll need to show them how getting you promoted is in their best interests–or better still, in the best interests of the company.

The thing to remember is that what you absolutely need is a mentor. Having a sponsor is optional, although it's definitely nice to have. Just don't confuse the two.

Of course, there are some circumstances in which people can act in both roles, but the key is to be clear with them and to set expectations. You both need to be on the same page from the outset, because if you expect them to sponsor you and they're only interested in acting as a mentor, you're bound to run into trouble. And if you're looking for someone to be a sponsor and your mentor can't do it, you need to go out and find someone else.

Be sure to make it clear that they can say no, just like you should if you ask someone for a letter of recommendation. Say something like, "I'd like for you to be my sponsor, but if you're not comfortable in doing so, please let me know and there'll be no hard feelings."

If they don't feel confident enough in your skills to recommend you for the job or the promotion then they need an out, otherwise they're not going to say no but they'll give you a lukewarm letter. Or they'll write you a letter of recommendation, but as soon as someone calls them up for verification, they'll say, "Well, actually…"

> ▷ **Action Item:** Take a look at the people in your network and identify those you think of as mentors and those you think of as sponsors. If you haven't done so already, take them out for a coffee and discuss your expectations of one another. Make sure that you're both on the same page and that you understand whether they're a mentor or a sponsor.

Your Teaching Teaches You

Most people tend to think that a person who's lived longer has experienced more in life and therefore has more to offer than a person who hasn't, but the truth is that they both have a lot to offer. The person with life experience has graduated from the school of hard knocks and carries the wisdom that comes from the failures and successes they've experienced along the way. However, they've also developed a certain amount of common sense, which isn't always a good thing.

Yes, common sense will tell you that the stove is hot and that you shouldn't put your hand on it. But it will also tell you, "This is the way that you should do things because this is the way that things have always been done." And the more experienced you get, the less you question the way things are.

Younger people haven't necessarily lived long enough or had enough experiences to develop this kind of common sense, and so they raise their hand and ask, "But why do we do it like that?"

Louis Braille lost his eyesight at the age of three and was constantly told by the adults around him that he'd never be able to read. But Braille didn't listen to common sense. Instead, he took a form of military code called "night writing" and made it much easier to use, allowing blind people all over the world to read and write when they'd otherwise be unable to.[13] He was unafraid to ask, "Why?"

---

[13] Chuvic, "You'll Never Believe These 28 Inventions Were Made by Kids," *Science Sensei*, December 12, 2024, https://sciencesensei.com/youll-never-believe-these-28-inventions-were-made-by-kids/

It's the "why" that keeps the mentor going, at least in my eyes, and that's the biggest gift that mentees have to offer. The way my mentees look at the world keeps me engaged and excited and allows me to think about what I'm doing in a different way. It gives me the motivation I need to continue and keeps me boarding that plane every few months to go back to Yale.

I've noticed that the same is true of my scientific work. When I speak to my peers, I tend to give talks that are at a high level, where I make a lot of assumptions about what people know. When I get questions, they tend to be detailed, specific questions about some arcane aspect or another, as opposed to more general questions about the general scheme of things and why we're doing what we're doing.

Then I started giving lectures where I talked to people who weren't experts in my field, and I soon discovered that I had to change the script completely. I couldn't assume that my audience knew anything or hide behind equations and big words. And it was only when I started to explain what I did to laypeople that I started to truly understand what I was actually doing.

It turns out that your teaching teaches you, just like when you mentor a student, your student ends up mentoring you, even if they don't realize it. A mentor can gain just as much as the mentee does. Frankly, it's because I've gained so much from my mentees that I continue to do what I'm doing.

It can also lead to other opportunities. For example, the mentee I mentioned who started an AI business presented me with a fantastic opportunity to invest in her startup. I know how she thinks and how hard she works, and so I'm fairly sure she's going to make a success of it, so I went ahead and invested. If I'm right, which I strongly suspect I will be, I'll get a monetary payback for something that I wasn't doing for the money.

The key is to do things like this because they're the right thing to do, and not with the expectation of a return. That way, anything that you do get will be a bonus.

Socks and Ties in the Interview Room

As a mentor, one of the most common questions you'll get is about how to prepare for an interview.

I used to just give people the conventional wisdom, like taking deep breaths to calm themselves down, but the students used to keep poking and prodding and asking questions that I couldn't answer. They said that taking deep breaths didn't work, and that it just made them look silly in the interview room. They also pointed out that if you're frightened of someone then taking a deep breath isn't going to work. You'll still be frightened; you'll just have a lung full of air. And you still wouldn't have answered their question.

Interviews are stressful situations. The interviewee is typically sitting alone across four or five strangers, doing everything they can to remain neutral. They're trying not to smile at you or to give you any cues of either encouragement or discouragement. Instead, they're maintaining a poker face, which makes it difficult to read what they're really thinking. To make matters worse, they're usually wearing nondescript clothing in a neutral color. That makes it even harder to make a guess at what their personality might be like, especially when you're stressed and unable to think clearly.

And so I told my students they should start reading the room. "Take a look at their socks and shoes or the ties they have on," I explained. "If they're wearing any jewelry, take a look at that. When we're in a formal situation, it's usually the accessories where we tend to express ourselves. Pick up on those small details and use them to try to create a mental image of what their personality might be like."

When you read the room like this in a formal situation, it makes the people you're talking to seem much more human, even when they're trying their hardest not to be.

If my mentees hadn't pushed me to go above and beyond my usual spiel, I wouldn't have started telling them what they really wanted to know. It's another great example of the mentees teaching the mentors, as well as when offering unconventional wisdom can be more beneficial than just echoing best practices.

Advice for Immigrants

Let's take a look at another example of how a mentor can learn from their mentees.

I was speaking on a panel with three other people to a group of students who were getting ready to graduate from Yale with science degrees. The other two were natural-born US citizens, and I was the only immigrant.

This is relevant because around three-quarters of the students in that room were immigrants or foreign students, and so they were thrilled that I was there. They were asking the panelists about their first jobs and what characteristics to look for, and the other three were saying that they should follow their passion. Then it was my turn to talk.

I leaned into the microphone and said, "Look, as an immigrant, if you're going to go from a student visa to a work visa then the most important thing to do is to find a job that will give you that visa. Otherwise, you could find the most amazing job in the world, but if they're not willing to support you for a visa then you're not going to be able to take it."

That was exactly the kind of advice they needed, and so after that, they kept on asking me questions because they wanted to know more. Plenty of people had told them what they should do, but they'd never talked about how to put it all into practice.

The lesson here is that if you want to help someone or to offer them advice, you need to know what they're looking for. In some cases, they'll be looking for very specific advice about very specific topics; in other cases, general advice will do. Sometimes, they just need you to listen while they chat through their ideas.

There are also times when people don't know what they're looking for, or when they think they're looking for one thing, but you realize from talking to them that they actually need something else.

It's like that apocryphal story about Henry Ford in which he's (falsely) reputed to have said, "If I'd asked people what they wanted, they would have said 'faster horses.'"[14]

On Multiple Mentors

Most people know that you don't need to have just one mentor and that you can have many of them. But I take that one step further.

Your goal should be to have mentors that play different roles in your life. You can have one mentor who can provide advice at work and another who can help you out at home. You can—and should—also take things to an even more granular level.

For example, it's helpful to have a mentor who works at the same company you do. They understand the organization's culture and can guide you on what it takes to be successful there. That's great, but they're not necessarily the person you want to talk to if you're having problems *with* the organization itself. After all, they might be

---

[14] quoteresearch, "Quote Origin: My Customers Would Have Asked For a Faster Horse," *Quote Investigator*, July 28, 2011, https://quoteinvestigator.com/2011/07/28/ford-faster-horse/

your colleague or your boss. They don't necessarily have your best interests at heart; they have their own priorities, and they also want to do what's best for the company. They might not give you good, impartial advice, and you might even end up getting into trouble.

That's why it can help to have a mentor who understands your industry but who doesn't work for your company. With them, you can talk about office politics without worrying that word will get back to your line manager.

You might also want a mentor who's in a completely different field, especially if you're thinking about switching careers and going from one role to another or even jumping ship to a different industry entirely. When that's the case, it's not helpful to talk to people in your own industry because they won't have much to offer you. People are naturally resistant to change and afraid of the unknown. They're going to tell you to just stick with what you're doing.

Of course, you might be lucky and be able to find someone in your industry who did something else before making the same kind of switch that you're thinking about doing. If so, they might be able to help you. But you usually don't have people's resumes or LinkedIn bios in front of you when you're talking to them, and so there's no way of knowing whether they've been in your industry for their entire career or whether they've only just made the switch.

Bear in mind that there are also skills that carry across from one industry to another. For example, if you need interview advice or help with your resume, it might not matter what industry your mentor is experienced in. If you're struggling with interpersonal skills or you're not sure how to handle someone who's being aggressive in a meeting and they're creating a hostile workplace, it doesn't really matter whether your mentor is an aerospace expert or a healthcare professional. As long as they've dealt with the same kinds of issues, they'll be able to help.

Going back to biases, don't forget that everyone in management will have biases, too. If you're having a problem with Steve but

Steve plays golf every weekend with his manager, are you going to take it up with them? Probably not. Are you going to take it up with the manager's manager? Maybe, but then Steve's manager might resent you for going over their head.

These are further examples of situations in which your first port of call should be someone from outside your organization. You shouldn't talk to your bosses about that unless you've talked to someone else first and done what you can to mitigate the situation. If that doesn't work, then you need to take it up with your superiors because you can't just let it fester like an infected wound. At the same time, you need to acknowledge that if you bring it up with the people in your organization, they might not take your side. You may even have to leave and search for work elsewhere, depending upon the office politics and how bad things get.

> ▷ **Action Item:** Revisit your list of mentors and sponsors and categorize them based upon the different areas that they can help you with. If in doubt, talk to them!

Why Not a Friend?

Now, you might be wondering whether you could just talk to a friend about this stuff. It's certainly an option, but it's not ideal. Remember, it's all about getting good, impartial advice, and your friends and family are anything but impartial. They're not objective because they love you. If you're not careful, you'll find yourself in an echo chamber.

When we talk to our friends and family, they're only getting one side of the story, which is our side. It's inherently biased. If we have a mentor who we know and respect but who we have an arm's length relationship with, they're more likely to probe and ask questions that make you think about things slightly differently.

I've noticed this when I talk to my wife about her work. Whenever she talks about someone who's behaving badly, I immediately take her side without even thinking. That's what you do when you love someone.

When I catch myself doing that, I force myself to ask the hard questions. She'll tell me that she was having a bad day because of a colleague, and I'll ask her whether it's really because of that person or whether it's because of something else. Often, her knee-jerk reaction is, "Why am I getting the third-degree when I'm the aggrieved party?"

That's why, when your partner starts complaining, you should ask them whether they want you to give them sympathy or whether they want you to give them advice, because those are two very different things. They might just want to complain, in which case your job is just to sit there and listen. If they want you to give them advice, you might have to ask them tough questions about things that they don't want to talk about. The key is to understand which of the two you're being asked to do and to make sure that you're both on the same page.

You should also consider the different roles that people play. A mentor's job is to provide you with advice, while it usually falls to your friends and family to comfort and support you. Additionally, bear in mind that once someone has been a mentor for several years, they might have developed a friendship with their mentee. When that's the case, it's time to have a chat and to determine whether it's time to move on and find another mentor.

It's the unbiased observers who'll ask the right questions, forcing you to tell your story while making sure that the other side is reflected. On top of that, the more impactful the decision is, the more important it is to get unbiased advice. If it's a question of where you're going to go for dinner, you can afford to take biased advice from someone with vested interests. If it's about whether or not to take a job that will require you to move to the other side of the country, you can't afford to take advice from someone who doesn't have your best interests at heart.

CHAPTER FOUR

Building a Virtuous Cycle

"I've learned that people will forget what you said, people will forget what you did, but people will never forget how you made them feel."

—Maya Angelou[15]

IF YOU GO TO WORK when you're unhappy, you're not going to do your best. And if you're not doing your best, people will say that you're not pulling your weight. That's going to aggravate you and make you hate your work even more, so you're going to put less effort in. Eventually, you'll either quit or get fired, and that's going to be the end of that.

On the other hand, if you're doing well and you're happy at work, you'll get lauded. You'll feel better and work harder, and that virtuous cycle will continue. It's a classic case of positive reinforcement: you do something good, you get a reward for it, and it makes you want to do even better next time. It becomes a spiral—either a positive one or a negative one, depending upon which direction you're going in.

The same thing happens when you meet people on the street. If you smile at them, they smile back at you. If you frown at them, they frown back at you. There was even an occasion where I smiled at someone and they turned around and said, "Thank you. I've been feeling terrible all day, but knowing there's still someone out there

---

[15] This quote is commonly attributed to Maya Angelou, but that attribution is unsupported. According to *Quote Investigator*, the earliest known appearance of a version of this quote is in a 1971 collection called *Richard Evans' Quote Book,* where it was credited to Carl W. Buehner.

who can smile made me feel like maybe I can, too." That was unexpected and not why I smiled at them, but it was also some positive reinforcement for greeting people when I walk.

There are some people who don't respond and just keep walking, and that's fine. I'm greeting them because it makes me feel good, and not because I want a reward from it. You do the right thing because it's the right thing to do, and not because you expect to get something in return.

Likewise, you can't go into mentoring with the expectation that you'll learn from the people you mentor. It's likely to happen anyway, but if it's the only reason why you're doing it, then you won't learn a thing.

Positive and Negative Cycles

To me, a cycle is something that causes something else to happen, usually in a way that becomes self-perpetuating. Rain falls from the sky, collects in lakes and rivers, evaporates, and condenses into clouds, and then the cycle begins all over again.

When most people think about cycles, their mind goes straight to the negative kind—the downward spiral. It's like the one we talked about at the start of this chapter: you wake up feeling awful, you go to work and you don't do very well, you go back home and fight with your family because you're in a bad mood. You sleep badly and have nightmares, and then you wake up still feeling miserable in the morning. You lash out again and do the same thing, and then the next thing you know, you're out of a job.

The virtuous cycle is basically its polar opposite. If you feel good in the morning, you tend to do better at work, and if you perform better at work, you might get a pat on the back from your boss before you leave. You head home happy, so you're nice to your loved ones and they're nice right back to you. You go to bed happy, and you wake up the next morning feeling rested, and the whole positive cycle begins again.

Of course, it's much easier to get into a virtuous cycle if the work you're doing excites you, and that's true whether you're doing something professionally or whether you're doing it voluntarily for the social good. It even applies to the work you're putting in to keep a relationship or a family going.

It all boils down to this: if you feel that what you're doing matters and makes a difference, and if it provides you with something more than just a paycheck, it'll help the virtuous cycle to continue.

When I was a graduate student, I saw a sign on a pin board beside the elevator that said that one of the professors was looking for a teaching assistant for an aerodynamics course for non-science majors. I found aerodynamics interesting, enjoyed looking at airplanes, and wanted to understand them a little more, and so I knocked on his door and asked him to tell me a little more about what the job entailed.

It turned out that I'd be going to various modeling and hobby shops to buy model airplanes which, when assembled, would be used to demonstrate the principles of aerodynamics. The fact that it was a course for non-science majors meant that there wouldn't be any numbers or equations and that it would all be taught by showing how things worked. The models were an important part of that.

Then he said, "Oh, I forgot to mention, but we'll make sure that you get paid."

I remember walking home that evening and pinching myself to make sure I wasn't dreaming. I couldn't believe it. "Did I just get offered a job where I'll be getting paid to do something that I'd save up my own money to do?" I wondered. "I must be the luckiest person on the planet."

It's a great example of how great it feels when your passion and your job are aligned with one another.

> ▷ **Action Item:** Spend some time taking a closer look at the cycles that you see in your own life. List as many as you can and categorize them as either positive or negative, then look for ways to break the negative cycles while perpetuating the positive ones.

Intrinsic versus Extrinsic Rewards

Writing for *Simply Psychology*, Harvard University research assistant Charlotte Nickerson explains, "Intrinsic motivation describes the undertaking of an activity for its inherent satisfaction, while extrinsic motivation describes behavior driven by external rewards or punishments, abstract or concrete. Intrinsic motivation comes from within the individual, while extrinsic motivation comes from outside the individual."[16]

If you're doing something because you enjoy it, because it's teaching you something, or because it feels worthwhile, you're motivated by intrinsic rewards. If you're only doing it for the money, you're motivated by extrinsic rewards.

We all need to make money to be able to live, but if we can make money while simultaneously receiving intrinsic rewards, we get the best of both worlds.

During the enforced isolation during the COVID-19 pandemic, I volunteered to go out and do the shopping. Nobody paid me for it, and so I didn't get any extrinsic rewards, but I did get the intrinsic rewards that came from chatting to some fellow shoppers and the people on the checkout counter. You can't put a price on that kind of human contact.

---

[16] Charlotte Nickerson, "Extrinsic vs. Intrinsic Motivation: What's the Difference?," June 19, 2025, *Simply Psychology*, https://www.simplypsychology.org/differences-between-extrinsic-and-intrinsic-motivation.html

True, I could have had the same conversations on Zoom, but it's not the same. Don't get me wrong, Zoom is fantastic, and it allows you to do all sorts of things that you wouldn't be able to do without it. But at the same time, we need to be in the presence of other human beings.

Recently, I took an overnight flight, arrived in New York, and then drove to Connecticut to go to Yale, where I attended meetings all day and then went out for drinks. By the time I went to bed, I'd been up from 6 a.m. to 3 a.m. the following morning, and I wasn't even tired. I was energized. Why? Because I'd spent the whole day in the company of people whose conversation I found stimulating.

People were amazed by the fact that I'd been able to stay awake, but the point was that I found it fun. I was even up for the next session at 8 a.m. the following morning, feeling perfectly rested because I'd had such a fantastic time. I wasn't motivated by a paycheck or some other kind of extrinsic reward. I was motivated by the intrinsic reward of the stimulating conversation I got from being in the company of like-minded people who I respected and admired. It's a great example of the power of virtuous cycles.

The opposite can be true, too. If it had been on my doorstep but I'd been there with people whose company I didn't enjoy and who I didn't find stimulating, I would have been in bed by 8 p.m. In fact, I've had that happen where we've had to host people and I've dearly wanted to crawl into bed. I was yawning and my wife was looking at me and saying, "Stop doing that, you're making the guests uncomfortable." But I couldn't help it!

> ▷ **Action Item:** Determine whether you're motivated more by intrinsic or extrinsic rewards.

The Power of the Virtuous Cycle

We've talked about the virtuous cycle for your work life and your personal life, but the virtuous cycle is just as valid when it comes to volunteering and doing things for the good of your community.

Let's say that you start going for a walk each day, and you carry a trash can and a litter picker with you. You pick up trash wherever you see it and then deposit it all in a trashcan on your way home. It makes you feel good because you've done your bit to make the neighborhood a better place.

Now let's say that you go out the next day, and you find that there's more trash than there was the day before. You're likely to feel dejected and to wonder why you even bothered. The chances are that you'll end up falling into a negative cycle. On the other hand, if you find that it's as clean or cleaner than it was, you're likely to feel intrinsically motivated to keep going.

Perhaps you keep on doing it, and then one day while you're out, you see another person picking up trash. They've seen the example that you have set and felt inspired to do the same thing. It's a virtuous cycle, and one that's contagious.

In other words, it's a meme.

Evolutionary biologist Richard Dawkins coined the term "meme" in his 1976 book, *The Selfish Gene*. Back then, it had nothing to do with internet culture like it does today. Dharmendra Jaiswal explains, "Dawkins defined a meme as an idea that spreads through imitation. This could be anything from a catchy tune to a fashion trend. These things spread because people copy each other. The key is that people mimic, or imitate, the idea."[17]

---

[17] Dharmendra Jaiswal, "The word 'meme' was invented in 1976, by Richard Dawkins. It means mimema in Greek, meaning 'imitated'.," *Storysilverbook*, March 13, 2025, https://storysilverbook.wordpress.com/2025/03/13/the-word-meme-was-invented-in-1976-by-richard-dawkins-it-means-mimema-in-greek-meaning-imitated/

The downside is that negative cycles can be memes, too. Think of all of the rock stars who followed their friends into the downward spiral of addiction. The lucky ones bounced back after hitting rock bottom. The unlucky ones are no longer with us.

When virtuous memes meet intrinsic motivation, you end up with a wave of positivity that spreads from one person to another. For example, when I started working with Butterflies and went back to visit the children after our first fundraising drive, they told me about all of the amazing things they'd been able to do thanks to our funding. It was amazing to see the joy in their eyes when they talked about what they'd learned and what their future held.

This intrinsic motivation made me want to redouble my efforts and to recruit even more like-minded people to the cause. I wanted to grow the organization so that we could help even more children to reach their full potential.

As for memes…well, that brings me back full circle to why I'm writing this book in the first place. It's my hope that people will read these stories, and that the meme will spread and inspire them to take action. The best-case scenario for me would be for you to come and join the charities that I'm working with, but an equally valid outcome is for you to ask yourself, "What can I do to impact my corner of the world—or a corner of the world that I feel particularly passionate about?"

The Power of Passion

Virtuous cycles are all well and good, but if you want to maintain the momentum and keep the cycle going, then you're going to need passion. After all, obstacles will always come along in life, no matter how you choose to live it. The thing to remember is that if you feel that what you're doing is worthwhile, you'll do whatever it takes to get past those obstacles.

I like to think of it as being like a marriage. If you think that your life partner is going to be 100 percent in sync with what you're thinking and that you're never going to have an argument, you're living in a utopian fantasy. In the real world, there are trials and tribulations—there will be little fights, and there might even be big ones. The key is to know whether it's worth the effort. If it is and you have that passion, you're going to survive and thrive. You'll wake up 40 years after marrying your sweetheart still feeling glad that you popped the question, instead of waking up and thinking, "Why am I here?"

Passion is what will get you past these obstacles, which is why I advise my students to try to find a career that they can be passionate about. Be conscious about what you're doing, and if you end up having three or four bad days in a row, sit down and take stock of what's going on. If there's a pattern there, and if that pattern is being caused because you're not interested or passionate about what you're doing, then you need to make a change. You're on the wrong path.

On the other hand, if the pattern is a result of external forces or the people that you're dealing with, you need to ask yourself, "Is it worth trying to address the issue and changing the situation?" Or are you not involved or committed enough to what you're doing to expend that effort?

Either way, when something isn't working, you need to think about what you're going to do to change things up, because just letting the status quo prevail isn't a good outcome. Sooner or later, it's bound to lead to failure. Three bad days will become six bad days, followed by a bad week, and then a bad month. Before you know it, it's affecting other aspects of your life.

The vicious and the virtuous cycles go hand in hand, and you need to be careful when you're riding the virtuous cycle to make sure that you don't fall off. It's much easier to go from the virtuous cycle to the vicious cycle than it is to go from the vicious cycle to the virtuous one.

This takes us full circle to aerodynamics, where you've got forward momentum versus gravity and wind resistance. A plane has to fly at a certain speed, otherwise it will fall from the sky. It also takes more energy to accelerate than it does to slow down.

Maintaining a virtuous cycle where every day leaves you feeling fulfilled takes conscious effort. Contentment won't just fall into your lap. That could only happen if we lived in a world without negativity, and unfortunately, I don't think that world exists today, I don't think it's ever existed, and I doubt very much that it ever will.

Writing for *How Stuff Works*, Jesslyn Shields explains, "You can't easily put the toothpaste back into the tube. You can't expect molecules of steam to spontaneously migrate back together to form a ball of water. If you release a bunch of corgi puppies into a field, it's very unlikely you're going to be able to get them all back together into a crate without doing a ton of work."[18]

This, in a nutshell, is the Law of Entropy, or the Second Law of Thermodynamics. The idea is that everything in our universe naturally tends to devolve towards chaos. You need to make a conscious effort and expend energy if you want to impose any form of order. If you spend a ton of time growing a rose garden, you need to maintain that garden by watering the plants and removing the weeds, or it will soon become overgrown as entropy kicks in.

Likewise, you need to make an effort if you want to get into and remain in a positive spiral. Otherwise, if you get into a positive spiral and stay neutral, that entropy will eventually drag you back down again, just like gravity and wind resistance on an airplane.

Ultimately, it's easy to forget what trajectory your life is on, and it's something that you'll have to keep course-correcting. Think of it like a satellite that's been launched into geosynchronous orbit,

---

[18] Jesslyn Shields, "Entropy: The Invisible Force That Brings Disorder to the Universe," *HowStuffWorks*, November 30, 2023, https://science.howstuffworks. com/entropy.htm

miles above the earth and outside its atmosphere. You still need to use its micro-thrusters to course-correct from time to time so that it doesn't come crashing back down to earth.

> ▷ **Action Item:** Identify what you're most passionate about and look for ways to funnel that passion into a virtuous cycle.

Staying on the Virtuous Cycle

So how do you stay on the virtuous cycle?

Well, I wish there was an easy answer to that. The best advice I can give you is that it all comes down to self-reflection, and that you need to commit to doing that self-reflection on a regular basis. I'd suggest every few days as a minimum.

How you do that is up to you. If you're the kind of person who likes Post-it notes, put one on your screen or on your refrigerator. If you prefer your calendar, put reminders in your calendar. Set reminders on your phone or on your watch. The specifics don't matter, as long as you've got something that forces you to proactively stop and say, "What am I doing? Why am I doing it?"

Personally, I rely on my iPhone and my Apple Watch. I've set it up so that the mindfulness app will ask me to log how I'm feeling once a day. I take that opportunity to log how I'm feeling and to reflect on why I'm feeling that way, which gives me an opportunity to identify what's going well and what isn't. Then I can figure out where I need to course-correct.

But that's not a one-size-fits-all recommendation. You have to use whichever method will work for you.

PART THREE

Transformative Impact

CHAPTER FIVE

Amandla in South Africa

"What is the use of living, if it be not to strive for noble causes and to make this muddled world a better place for those who will live in it after we are gone?"

–Winston Churchill[19]

I WAS SUPER PROUD of the videos we'd made at Butterflies, and I wasn't afraid to show them to my friends and acquaintances to give them an idea of what I was doing and maybe to even raise some money for the charity along the way.

And so most of the people I knew had a good idea of what I was doing at Butterflies, including the then-executive director of the Yale Alumni Association, Weili Chang. She'd been chatting with a fellow graduate called Scott Clarke, and she thought the two of us should talk. Scott is originally from Jamaica, but he grew up in Miami and New York, went to school at Yale, and ended up settling in Cape Town, South Africa after seeing some of the issues there and deciding to stick around to help tackle them. That was how Amandla was born.

Scott was in a bit of a quandary, wondering how to raise funds in the US and how to set up a board of directors that could help him to achieve his fundraising goals. He'd been talking to Weili, and she'd said, "There's this guy called Rahul who's been working hard to raise money for an Indian charity called Butterflies. You should talk to him. He might be able to give you some pointers."

---

[19] "Quotes Falsely Attributed to Winston Churchill," *International Churchill Society*, accessed October 10, 2025, https://winstonchurchill.org/resources/quotes/quotes-falsely-attributed/

We met in 2018 at a small café in San Francisco. Every time I drive by on First Street, I take a look at the multi-colored chairs on its patio, and it takes me back to that wonderful, hour-and-a-half conversation we had. We were only supposed to talk for 45 minutes.

I basically did a data dump and told Scott everything I could think of that I'd learned from my work with Butterflies, including what had been most successful when it came to raising funds. When I finished, he turned to me and said, "You know, Rahul, you've imparted so much knowledge that it's been difficult for me to absorb it. It's like drinking from a firehose. Can I ask for your help to create this board? And would you mind being its founding president?"

That little word "yes" popped out of my mouth, and the rest, as they say, is history. I helped him found the board, recruiting board members who'd all visited Amandla in person. That happened because the Yale Alumni Association has an interesting program called the Yale Alumni Service Corps, or YASC. They partner with charities all over the globe and organize service trips for people to go and visit them. A couple dozen Yale alumni will travel to the location, often with their families, to volunteer. They'll live in modest accommodation and pay their own way as they volunteer with the organizations.

Scott had been involved with the YASC for a while and had already arranged for a couple of trips to go out to Amandla, which was how we were able to find people to join the board. Around a hundred Yale alumni had travelled out across a couple of different trips, and they all came back feeling super excited about the work that Amandla does. That made our work a lot easier.

Starting Small

When I started working with Amandla, we started off relatively small, collecting around $35,000 in the first year. As of 2024, we're at just under a quarter of a million dollars annually. That's pretty good considering that we couldn't do much during the first year because COVID shut everything down. We were still able to host board meetings online, but that was about it.

Sending anything other than money to South Africa was impossible because as part of their response to COVID, South Africa had restricted any goods from entering the country. Everything that arrived there got stuck at the ports, and so while we could have shipped out masks, hand sanitizers, and COVID tests, we realized that there wasn't any point because it would have arrived in Cape Town and then just sat there in a shipping container.

I was supposed to visit Amandla in March 2020, but the pandemic forced us to postpone the trip until January 2022, when my wife and I flew over to Cape Town. Amandla is based in Philippi, which is a shanty town with a bad reputation. Scott had warned us not to tell our Uber driver that we were going to Philippi, because that's a sure-fire way to get them to refuse the trip.

I took Scott's advice, and so while I entered the street address in the app, I didn't directly address it with the driver. He seemed happy enough to take us, but when we were almost there, he realized where we were headed. He turned around to us and said, "No, I can't take you there. It's a very dangerous place. They dig potholes in the roads to trap drivers, and there are people just sitting in the street, watching you. If the car gets stuck in a pothole, they'll show up with guns and rob us both. I can't take you."

I called Scott and told him what had happened, and he told me to ask the Uber driver to drop me off at the police station just outside Philippi so that he wouldn't have to go inside the township. The driver did so, and Scott came along and picked us up from there.

My first impressions were that Philippi wasn't as bad as everyone said it was. Yes, there were potholes, but there are potholes in every city in the world. They certainly hadn't been dug up by criminals, and they weren't big enough for a car to get stuck in. That was one myth debunked, so let's take a look at the second one.

It's true that everyone was sitting outside, but that's because they live in tin shacks. Most of them are transportation containers, the kind that you see on ocean liners. They have doors cut out of them, and if they're lucky, they also have a window.

Imagine living in one of those containers when it's 100°F. Who's going to sit inside? It would be like sitting inside an oven. People sit outside in Philippi because they *have* to, and if they're sitting outside, what are they supposed to do—not look at you?

Scott took us to one of the safe spaces and introduced us to some of the staff. The safe spaces are scattered throughout Philippi, and my wife and I visited four of them during our visit to Cape Town. We were accompanied in our travels by two young women, one was a volunteer and the other was working there. That meant there were four of us: two obvious foreigners and two young women. In short, we were prime targets. And yet, we spent the whole day there and not a single soul bothered us.

The whole myth of Philippi being a dangerous place was just that: a myth. Just because someone happens to be poor and under-privileged, it doesn't mean that they're a criminal.

Call and Response

The word *Amandla* comes from a rich tradition of African call and response. In many African folk songs, the primary singer calls out and then the chorus responds. The call and response *Amandla* is part of that, and while its meaning can be translated in different ways, Scott defines it as "the power is ours."[20]

---

20 "From the Founder," Amandla Development, accessed October 10, 2025, https://amandladevelopment.org/from-the-founder.

Writing for *Elephant Journal*, Bianca Marks says, "I grew up in Apartheid South Africa. Protest was an almost daily occurrence. People were frustrated and they wanted their freedom. 'Amandla Awethu' was a phrase commonly used during the struggle. The leader of a group would call out 'Amandla!' and the crowd would respond with 'Awethu'. This literally means: power to the people!"[21]

As an organization, Amandla uses the term in the context that we have the power to change, to provide help for the children of Philippi from cradle to college. This requires a holistic approach that touches every part of their lives. For example, Amandla provides people with food so that they can get enough to eat and actually concentrate on their studies. After all, at any given time, about half of all of kids living in Philippi are undernourished.

A significant fraction of the kids in Philippi are born with HIV/AIDS. Unfortunately, the girls are in a worse situation than the boys, probably because of the way in which AIDS is transmitted through the genes from parents who have it.

Over 90 percent of cases of childhood HIV infections are due to transmission from infected mothers during pregnancy, childbirth, or breastfeeding. Writing for *Medical News Today*, Robby Berman notes, "HIV hits children particularly hard, since their young immune systems can't fight infections as well as those of adults. These children experience various subsequent health issues, including ear and sinus infections, sepsis, pneumonias, tuberculosis, urinary tract infections, intestinal illness, skin disease, and meningitis."[22]

---

[21] Bianca Marks, "Power to the People : Nelson Mandela Quotes I Live By," *Elephant Journal*, April 30, 2015, https://www.elephantjournal.com/2015/04/power-to-the-people-nelson-mandela-quotes-i-live-by/
[22] Robby Berman, "Why are cases of HIV infections on the rise among girls?," *Medical News Today*, December 22, 2023, https://www.medicalnewstoday.com/articles/why-are-cases-of-hiv-infections-on-the-rise-among-girls

All of this means that the kids need to be tested, and if they test positive, then they need to learn how to live with the condition and how to beat the odds.

They also need to be helped with their schoolwork, because most of the adults are illiterate and they look at their children as sources of money—another pair of hands that could be put to work to bring in a little income. They don't realize that if their kids get an education, they'll be able to get better jobs and they'll be able to better take care of their parents and their families in the long run.

And let's not forget that it's often just a case of providing kids a safe space—a place where they can be children for a while, free from the pressure of being told they're wasting their time studying or playing when they could be working. After all, they're still just kids, some as young as eight and others barely eighteen.

The Role of Research

The Amandla program is going from strength to strength, and Philippi is now home to six safe spaces serving 50,000 students every year. The plan is to expand that even further and to go beyond Philippi to other townships.

We wouldn't be able to do this without the support of the local community, but we also get a lot of help from the government. In fact, the government has started to ask for Amandla's help when it comes to partnering with other programs so that they can learn from us and make those other programs as successful as Amandla has been.

Amandla has a reputation for being good at record-keeping because they keep written records of every interaction with every child. They've been able to get a bunch of grants because there are a lot of researchers out there who want to study the effects of environmental factors on childhood development. Amandla's record-keeping allows them to partner with researchers and research organizations, bringing in additional revenue to keep the program going. It also brings in experts who can make sure that the kids get what they need.

We now have kids who've graduated from the program and come back to work at Amandla because it's changed their lives, just like Butterflies has changed lives in India. They want to make sure that they can provide the same opportunities that they had to the next generation, because otherwise they'll never break the cycle of discrimination.

After all, the shanty towns were created as a direct result of apartheid, and while over thirty years have passed since it ended in 1994, its ugly legacy remains.[23] The shanty towns might not be as racially motivated as they were in the past, but there are still huge socioeconomic strands for us to tackle.

The Book Club

One of the things about Amandla that's sparked the most joy for me has been the virtual book club that we've created. Some of our board members read the book here in the US, which also helps to keep the board members engaged with the students and to make sure that they see the positive effects of the work that Amandla is doing.

I'll never forget that first book club meeting. The kids had all gathered together in the one big room they had in the safe space, and they had a single computer with Zoom on it. We'd read an age-appropriate children's book on basketball and the two board members who were the chaperones of the book club started asking the kids some questions about it.

Kids are the same the world over, and as always happens in these kinds of situations, they started out completely silent. Then one of

---

[23] Robert Longley, "The End of South African Apartheid," *ThoughtCo*, May 17, 2022, https://www.thoughtco.com/when-did-apartheid-end-43456

the kids raised his hand. That took a lot of guts–not because he had to speak up, but because he had to get up and come closer to the computer so that we could hear them.

After that first kid started talking to us, the ice was broken, and the others couldn't wait to tell us what they'd thought of the book. This takes me full circle to the idea that mentors can learn from their mentees. The kids were looking at the book in a totally different way than the two of us sitting in the US.

After the book club was over, we ended the call with the kids and then got on the phone with one another. As we dissected the session, it came to us that while we were happy that we'd been able to do something for the kids, we were also happy that we'd done it for ourselves. It gave us some insights into the children's lives and how much of a difference Amandla was making.

Fifteen Years of Amandla

Amandla has been around for fifteen years now, and we're hoping to grow it over the next three or four years to take it to the next level, from 50,000 students a year to 250,000. The plan is to expand outside of Philippi into other shanty towns, first in Cape Town and then to the other big cities throughout South Africa. Next up: Johannesburg.

There are plenty of other organizations that do similar work to Amandla, but they're not as effective because they don't have the same grassroots approach to things. Unlike Amandla, they don't involve the local community or the government. People are taking note of the great work that Amandla is doing and the results that they're getting, and so they want to learn how to follow in their footsteps.

Before Scott launched Amandla in Philippi, only 20 percent of eighteen-year-olds in the area were going to college. That number is significantly larger now, mostly because of the efforts of Amandla.

We've been able to create a virtuous cycle through word of mouth about what Amandla is doing for the children. If you visit one of the safe spaces after school lets out, you'll find a bunch of the regular kids who always come along, and there will almost always be some new kids–their classmates and their schoolmates–who've been convinced to come along because it's a cool place to hang out.

They love to play soccer, but there are plenty of other activities, too. They stage plays and musicals to increase community involvement, a strategy that clearly works. That was evident as we travelled from safe space to safe space, because our two guides were greeted by people wherever we went.

They were known because they reached out to the community, and that's an important part of why Amandla works. You can't help people whose parents don't want you to help them; if you tried, you'd end up in an "us versus them" situation. If that happened, the parents would put their feet down and tell their children that they aren't allowed to spend time in the safe spaces anymore. The kids would have to obey because they can't just walk away and decide to leave home. Where would they go?

Changing Attitudes

Amandla already faces an uphill struggle when it comes to making change happen out in the world, but just as importantly, they have to change people's attitudes. That means changing the kids' attitudes towards what's possible for them in their future, changing their parents' attitudes towards education, and even changing attitudes throughout society as a whole.

Amandla's mission won't be over until people like the Uber driver I met have a completely different attitude towards Philippi and the people who call it home. If he'd come with us instead of refusing to drive into the township, he would have seen for himself that it's not a dangerous place. The people who live there are just ordinary people who happen to be living in extreme poverty. That's not their fault—they were born into it, and nobody is helping them to get out of it.

Even if it's a high crime area, we should remember that crime exists in every area of society—it just manifests differently. When there's a crime in an area like Philippi, it's driven out of desperation, rather than greed. They're stealing food because they need to eat, rather than stealing money so they can buy a vacation home and a nicer car.

Changing people's attitudes takes time, but the work that we're doing in South Africa is going to help us to make a change. It might take years, rather than months, weeks, or days, but that's okay. As long as we can get the ball rolling and see some results, we'll be happy. It's amazing to see people who are living in the shanty towns get an education and go on to work in the city. When that happens, they're usually able to find better accommodation for their families, so that they don't have to live in such poverty. Some of them even come back and work in places like Amandla, helping to drive that virtuous cycle of upward mobility.

We're doing what we can to help that cycle, too. For example, we're trying to partner with a Dutch energy company that wants to build solar farms in South Africa. They need a trained workforce, so we're in talks for them to provide us with some funding so that we can set up a training program to train the locals. That way, they can work in the factories to build the solar panels or assemble them on roofs and in solar farms. The young people of Philippi get good jobs, and the company saves money by using a local workforce instead of importing people from elsewhere.

It multiplies the goodness. Switching to solar is already a good thing, and if you can do that while driving positive social change, then everybody wins. The company could purchase solar panels from elsewhere and import them, then install them with an international workforce. That would be great from an energy perspective, but it's not great from a social perspective because the only jobs being created would be for foreigners.

The Holistic Approach

This holistic approach towards solar power echoes what Amandla is all about. They don't just provide meals or a safe space; they provide everything that the kids need to survive and thrive. You can't just tackle a single symptom; you've got to tackle all of the symptoms and the cause at the same time. If you want to effect lasting change, that's vital.

Providing food or a safe space alone would be a Band-Aid solution. It's better than nothing, but it also leaves a lot undone.

Our aim is to make sure that everyone in Philippi is given a chance to graduate from high school. If they want to go to college afterwards, they should have the chance to do that, too. The problem is that if you don't have food, shelter, and other necessities, you won't survive long enough to graduate from high school in the first place. That's why we need a holistic approach.

As part of that, we make sure that there are rooms available with air conditioning so that there's somewhere they can go to sit indoors and do their homework without baking under the South African sun. There are desks and chairs, as well as both volunteers and paid staff who can help them with their homework if they're getting stuck.

It's important to make sure that there's always someone there to ask for help because they probably won't be able to ask their parents. The chances are that their parents are unable to read and write, and the only answer that they'll get is, "See, they're not even teaching you anything at school, so why are you wasting your time there? Why don't you go out and get a job like everyone else?"

Our next step is to raise more money by getting more people involved in the US so that we can help to expand Amandla. As part of that, we're looking for new board members who can help us to achieve our larger financial goals.

One of the things that I'm positive about is that everyone who joins the board should make every effort to take their own personal trip to South Africa. Anyone can give money to the cause, and every dollar helps, but if you want to be a true champion of the cause, then it's much better to take a trip to Cape Town and to visit the kids in Philippi.

Meet the kids and listen to their voices. They get super excited when people ask them what makes them tick and how they spend their time. One begins to speak, and before you know it, they're all at it. You have to hush them and make them wait their turn so that they all get a chance to speak.

It's always important to go back to the source, which is why it's better to hear from the kids and not from the counselors and support staff who help them. It makes all of the difference in the world.

CHAPTER SIX

Amplifying Trust

"Trust is the glue of life. It's the most essential ingredient in effective communication. It's the foundational principle that holds all relationships."

—Stephen R. Covey

ONE OF THE THINGS I've noticed during my travels to Amandla and Butterflies is that the organizations have the power to change the way that the children look at themselves.

During my first visit to Butterflies, I was amazed by how the children seemed to be enjoying themselves. After all, they'd all been separated from their parents, either because they wanted to be separated or because they were lost. Being separated from your parents is a traumatic experience, and it's difficult to track missing parents down, especially in populous cities like the ones in India. Every attempt was being made, of course, but in the meantime, Butterflies was doing its best. In spite of everything, the children seemed to be enjoying themselves. They were flourishing.

On a subsequent trip, I talked to a group of the children who were working at the Khazana. I asked one of them what their role was, but I wasn't expecting him to turn around and say, "I'm the bank manager." He said it with such pride that I couldn't help smiling. Here's a kid that doesn't have an address, who spends his days and nights in a slum somewhere. He can't open a regular bank account, and yet because of Butterflies, he'd been given the opportunity to become a bank manager. Initiatives like the Khazana can create a huge feeling of empowerment amongst the children.

The other question that I asked them was, "How did you come to be at Butterflies?" Almost every single one of them said that a friend that had encouraged them to come along, and in most cases, those friends weren't even in the room.

This kind of peer-to-peer recruitment is vital for the program to work, because the kids are in an environment in which their parents aren't necessarily going to encourage them to go along to the safe spaces. Generally speaking, the parents can't even read or write and don't see the value of education. If kids weren't bringing their friends along, it would be much more difficult for these organizations to reach new people.

Testing for AIDS and COVID

When Amandla was first getting started, hardly anyone in Philippi was getting tested for AIDS because for that to happen, they'd have to visit a government hospital, where the first thing they'd be asked would be, "Well, what have you been up to? And why do you need to be tested?" That automatically puts the blame on the child, who's blameless in that situation.

Amandla found a way to change all of that by partnering with the government and taking over the testing, bringing it into the safe spaces so that the kids can get tested in a more welcoming environment. When they're tested at Amandla, nobody asks them why they need testing—they just give them the test. They're also given ways in which to prevent HIV/AIDS in the first place and taught how they can get treatment if they're infected.

As a result of this, when the COVID-19 pandemic came along, the children came to Amandla in droves, asking to be tested for COVID. As soon as the government made testing kits available, Amandla started to offer them. Before long, over 90 percent of people in Philippi were getting tested, because they trusted Amandla and had confidence in the organization's ability to deliver what they promised.

That gave Philippi a much higher testing rate than most of the rest of the world, both in developed and developing countries. That's understandable, because people were suspicious–they didn't have trust in the people administering the tests. There were theories that it was all a conspiracy to take advantage of people. There were even rumors that there were microchips in the vaccines.[24]

For Amandla, perhaps the most interesting thing that came out of the COVID-19 pandemic was the fact that when the kids came to get tested, they also brought their parents, their aunts and uncles, their grandparents, and their other friends and family members. The testing rate was only being held back by the number of tests that they had available, as opposed to the number of people who wanted to be tested.

The same thing happened when it came to vaccinations. Amandla was able to use the trust that they'd built up within the community to deliver vaccinations. When we started offering HIV testing at the safe spaces, we talked to the health officials and offered them a deal. Carrying out the testing was such a mundane task that they could train our laypeople to administer the tests, rather than taking up time that nurses could be using to take care of patients and save lives.

The healthcare workers weren't doing anything wrong, of course. It's just that we knew we could take a weight off their shoulders, and they were more than happy to let us. Meanwhile, the people of Philippi felt more comfortable being vaccinated by the people of Amandla. Everybody won.

That led to another great example of a virtuous cycle in which trust built upon trust. You have to be careful with this kind of thing, because if you make a mistake, then you lose a lot of the trust that you've built up. Our primary goal has always been to help the

---

24 Flora Carmichael and Jack Goodman, "Vaccine rumours debunked: Microchips, 'altered DNA' and more," *BBC News*, December 2, 2020, https://www.bbc.co.uk/news/54893437

children of Philippi, and if we messed up the vaccinations, word would travel, and the kids would have stopped coming.

It's a lot quicker and easier to lose trust than it is to gain it. In many ways, it's like a romantic relationship. It can take you months or even years to earn the deep trust of your partner, and if you're unfaithful to them, that's it–they'll never trust you again. You won't just lose the trust; you'll also lose the potential to regain it. They'll start to be suspicious whenever anything out of the ordinary happens. Their minds will always go back to the time you cheated on them, and they'll look at everything through that lens going forward.

Maintaining Trust

Butterflies and Amandla have both worked long and hard to build trust amongst the children they serve. That's why we've taken the approach of ensuring that the US arms never tell head office what approaches to take or how to do what they do. We'd rather leave that to the people who live in the country because they're the ones who understand the situation and the culture and they're also the ones who've built up trust with the local population.

There's be no point in us stepping in and saying, "You need to do it this way because that's how we do it in the US." For a start, we might be suggesting that they do things that are impractical because of the amount of resources it would take. That would only create a situation where we're at loggerheads with the very people we're trying to help.

Take the Khazana at Butterflies. They keep their books in an old-fashioned ledger, which they write in with a pen. We could tell them that they need to use a laptop, but we don't. Why? Well, for a start, it would cost more money, because they'd have to have a laptop, as well as a backup for when the laptop inevitably malfunctions.

We've tried to structure things in such a way that if the team in India decides that it would be best to use laptops, they could come to us and ask for funds. But we'd never do things the other way around and tell them, "This is how you should be doing things." At the end of the day, they're the experts.

Also, bear in mind that all of the children have been taught how to read and write, and they all know how to use a paper and pencil. As soon as you plug a laptop in, you've created a hierarchy, because there are some kids who know how to use computers and there are others who don't.

The minute you create that sort of inequality, you're also creating mistrust. The kids who don't know anything about the laptop will say, "Wait a second. I brought you 100 rupees, and you said you were going to add them to my account. But how can I be sure that they've been added?" As long as the kids know how to read and write, they can look at the ledger and see that their account has been updated. That's not necessarily the case when you're using a laptop.

Those of us who've been using laptops for decades tend to implicitly trust them, but that blind trust can be problematic because if you mistype something then the results come out wrong. Often, you take them at face value and trust that the results are right because that's what the computer says.

I remember this happening many years ago, before digitalization was as widespread as it is today. Back then, if you went to the store, the products would have stickers with their price on, and the cashier had to manually enter the prices into the cash register. The cashier added up five items that were all worth a couple of dollars or so, and when she finished ringing it all up, she told me I owed her $102.

"That doesn't make any sense," I replied. "I was expecting it to cost about twenty bucks."

We sat down together, and I went through the addition with her. When we tried it again, it came out to around $18. My guess is that she entered an extra zero somewhere.

As another example of maintaining trust by trusting the locals, let's say that you're providing food. If you're doing it the American way, you might offer hamburgers and fried chicken, but India has more vegetarians than any other country in the world, and even those who eat meat aren't going to want to eat beef because of their religion.[25, 26] That's why McDonald's uses chicken for their equivalent of the Big Mac at their 421 franchises in India.[27] The flavors are different, too. The same is true at Pizza Hut, where you can find yourself eating tandoori food on a pizza. And that's necessary if they want to succeed.

Long before McDonald's launched espressos in the US, some of the best espresso that you could get in France was at McDonald's. I was in Bordeaux one year and McDonald's was the only place that was open because it was six o'clock in the morning. I was desperately craving coffee and so I thought I'd give them a chance. You could have knocked me over with a feather when I tasted it. It was *good*.

And it's all because they have a financial incentive to meet the market.

[25] Kriti Barua, "Which Country Has the World's Largest Vegetarian Population? See Which Nation Tops the List!" *Jagranjosh.com*, December 30, 2024, https://www.jagranjosh.com/general-knowledge/list-of-countries-with-largest-vegetarian-population-1735565290-1

[26] Wendy Doniger, "Hinduism and its complicated history with cows (and people who eat them)," *The Conversation*, July 17, 2017, https://theconversation.com/hinduism-and-its-complicated-history-with-cows-and-people-who-eat-them-80586

[27] Parina Sood, "McDonald's India (W&S) aims to reach 580 to 630 restaurants by 2027," *FranchiseIndia.com*, April 7, 2025, https://www.franchiseindia.com/insights/en/news/mcdonalds-india-ws-aims-to-reach-580-to-630-restaurants-by-2027.56186

Cooperative Learning

Another way that Butterflies is building trust with the youth of New Delhi is via cooperative learning.

The kids at the contact centers can't be separated by grade when they're doing their homework because there isn't enough space. They have to be clustered together, no matter what grade they're in. That might sound like a problem, but we've been able to turn it into an opportunity.

The idea behind cooperative learning is to let the children help each other, so that the ones who are further along can help the ones who are trailing behind. Of course, we make sure that there are volunteers around who can help out, but we find that the kids learn better when they're learning from their friends instead of from a teacher or a figure of authority.

The idea has worked so well that it's been adopted by other children's health organizations in other parts of India. Why? Because they trust the data that we've collected. Yet again, it's a case of the amplification of trust. Other charities and organizations are looking at what we're doing and saying, "Butterflies is doing a great thing, and we trust the way they're doing it. Let's try and duplicate it."

Of course, they won't do things in exactly the same way, because different states have different requirements. The language and culture might be different, but the overall structure will remain the same. They say that imitation is the greatest form of flattery, and it's much better than an outsider going in and saying, "This is the way you should teach your kids."

The cooperative learning approach isn't much different from the Montessori method, which has been around in the West for decades. But if we'd gone in and told them to use the Montessori method, it wouldn't have gone down well. We've had much more success by allowing them to discover cooperative learning for themselves.

Something similar is happening in South Africa, where the government is keeping a close eye on how we're attracting the ever-increasing number of kids that live in Philippi to attend our safe spaces. They've been telling organizations working in other shanty towns in other cities to take a look at what we're doing and to find ways to adapt it for their own locations because it's such a successful model.

Trust is built one person at a time, whether you're just starting out or have been around for a decade or more. If you're starting a new organization, you can't expect everyone to trust you from day one. Some people will, of course, but it might take others years or even decades.

Remember that even when people are up against a tough situation, they don't necessarily want to be guinea pigs in someone's experiment. There will always be people who want to be at the cutting edge of things; if they're suffering and there's a new treatment, they'll be happy to test it because anything is better than what they're enduring. Other people will say, "Hey, I don't know if it's safe. I'm not going to try it until plenty of other people have tried it and nothing bad has happened to them."

> ▷ **Action Item:** Look for cooperative learning opportunities in your own life. Don't be afraid to reach out to people in your network and to offer them some of the insights you've uncovered with no expectation of reciprocation. The idea is to cultivate an environment of knowledge sharing and mutual advancement.

The Leap of Faith

We all have things we're willing to do easily and things where it requires more of a leap of faith. If someone tells you about a great job opportunity, you might be hesitant to apply for it because you're settled where you are. If it's working for you, why make a change?

You have to be willing to take a risk, even though that also means that you open yourself up to the possibility of failure. The key is to find the least risky way of taking that shot, which can often mean doing something in your spare time. That's often how entrepreneurs get their start.

When it comes to making big changes, it's easy to get overwhelmed by the fact that you find yourself in fresh surroundings, applying a new set of skills to a completely different set of circumstances. Starting out slowly can help you to judge your comfort level and to get some clarity so that you're sure that you're moving towards the right direction. It's all about building trust in yourself, because if you don't trust yourself, how can you ever hope to make a change?

As human beings, we tend to forget that every single thing we've done in our lives has required us to first take a huge leap of faith. When you were a baby, you could only lie there, at least until you learned how to roll over. Then, one fine day, you got the idea that you could push yourself up on to your hands and knees. You learned to crawl.

Before you knew it, you were standing up. You took a step, faltered, took another step and faltered again, and eventually, you started walking. That then led to running. Along every step of this journey (pun intended), you did something that you'd never done before.

The first time you spoke, you'd never spoken before. When you learned how to read, you'd never read before. If you've ever learned to speak a different language, you'd never done that before. When you learned that 1+1=2, you'd never done that before. These are all huge achievements.

By the time that you enter the workforce, your life has already been filled with all manner of firsts, even if you didn't necessarily celebrate them or receive a medal for achieving them. You have to learn to recognize that you're capable of doing things outside of your comfort zone because you've done it so many times before.

In a roundabout way, this takes me back to the "Where Do I Go from Yale?" program that I started with the Graduate School Alumni Association. The whole point of that program was to give PhD students more self-confidence. They started a research project without knowing much about it, and by the time they finished their PhD, they were the world's foremost expert on that topic. They'd solved a problem that nobody else had ever solved before.

There just aren't that many jobs in academia, and so we wanted to show that they could enter the workforce. Just because you're an academic, it doesn't mean you have to become a professor. If your field is English literature, instead of becoming a teacher, you could become a librarian. The possibilities are endless, as long as you have trust in yourself.

The same is true if you want to change your career. Perhaps you've achieved a lot and experienced some success but feel like something is missing. If you can figure out what that missing thing is, you can take the next step, which is to determine how to best fill that gap.

In my case, I filled the gap by helping underprivileged children, but I first had to recognize that there was something I could do. It all started when I translated and narrated a video that reached a wide audience and inspired people to donate. I sent the video to my friends and family, asking them if they recognized the narrator and encouraging them to donate if they were able to. That therefore amplified the effect of my work, but I had to trust myself first.

I'd never narrated a video before, but I had faith in my ability to do so. Once we started, I realized I could actually do it, and that pushed me forward. After that, I ended up recording segments for the alumni association and for some of the other organizations I've been involved with. Every time I do it, someone behind the camera says, "Do you do this professionally?"

If only they knew the truth.

The Bank Manager

Let's go back to the kid who was the bank manager at the Khazana in New Delhi. They had to trust themselves and believe that they had what it took to be the bank manager, which couldn't have been easy, considering the circumstances they were raised in. It was likely Butterflies that gave them that self-confidence in the first place.

The great thing about trusting yourself is that this creates another one of those virtuous cycles that we've talked about. Having become the bank manager at the Khazana, they gave themselves the gift of self-trust that comes from knowing that they can do the job. And if they can run the Khazana, perhaps they can be the first kid in their family to go to college and help to get their family out of poverty.

I daresay that the kid who introduced himself to me as the bank manager wouldn't have a problem walking into a bank and asking for a job. If he got it, he'd be so thrilled to have a job that he'd do everything he could to excel at it. It wouldn't take him long to rise through the ranks to become a bank manager because he's already got the confidence that comes from having done it once before. To me, that's a huge amount of empowerment being provided to these kids by Butterflies, because it's giving them a sense of self-worth.

There's a video that's being produced by Amandla which features a young woman who came to the safe space as a child. She talks about how she felt before she got there. She was upset and depressed, and she didn't think her life had any meaning. It wasn't until she came to Amandla and made friends with the other children that she was able to find some purpose.

After discovering the friendly, supportive adults at Amandla, she said that her days became different, and she'd learned how to smile. She then gave this little smile that brought tears to my eyes.

She's got a beautiful smile, and one that she'd never known how to use.

She only trusted the organization because we'd worked for so long to build that trust—and when I say "we," I really mean the organization, because as I said, we in the US don't believe in trying to do the local work without their input. We're happy to go there and help out, but we're observers as opposed to participants.

The people on the ground know that the people in the US have got their backs, and they can trust us to do that without stepping in and trying to take over. They'll come to us with a problem and ask us how we'd go about tackling it, and we'll always preface our answer with, "This is what we'd do in the US, but just remember that it's only valid for the States. We have no idea whether it's valid elsewhere." That's what makes us different from the missionaries, because we're not out there trying to proselytize people.

Trust builds success and success builds trust. That makes it another great example of the virtuous cycles that we've talked about.

Tools for Action

CHAPTER SEVEN

Turning Passion into Purpose

"The people who are crazy enough to think they can change the world are the ones who do."

— Steve Jobs[28]

ONE OF THE most important things that I've learned throughout the years is that if you're passionate about something, you can achieve a lot with your passion. When you're passionate, you get excited, and when you get excited, you put in 110 percent of your effort. You give it everything you have.

When I find a cause that I'm passionate about, I like to dip my toes in to see how I can make a difference. That allows me to see if there's a possibility for me to actually move the needle. If there isn't, my time might be better spent elsewhere.

It's true that no single individual can change the world, but if we sit back and take that at face value, why bother trying? The truth is that while no one can change the whole world, we all have the power to change the small part of the world that's closest to us.

I've also found that when you're passionate about something, your passion bleeds through when you speak about it to other people. Your excitement and enthusiasm become infectious, and before you know it, instead of having one person that's passionate about the project, you have two, and then four, and so on. It multiplies, like grains of rice on a chessboard in the ancient Indian

---

[28] Apple Archive, "Think Different – Steve Jobs (1997) – Apple," *YouTube*, https://youtu.be/CLIyH2SyxZA?si=ddFlgjdkyvdHnglk

legend.[29] That also allows you to surround yourself with people who share in your enthusiasm and who'll work with you to make your dream a reality.

There's a clear example with Amandla, where I started on the ground floor. Scott Clark already had the passion and had dedicated his life to setting up the program. He had funding for it from South African sources and some US sources as well, long before he even met me. His dream was to take Amandla to the next level so that instead of influencing the lives of a fraction of the kids, he was improving the lot of every child that lived in Philippi. Eventually, he wants to go beyond Philippi to some of the other shanty towns throughout South Africa to raise the standard of living and education for all South African youth, and not just those who live locally.

To do that requires a lot of planning and resources, but Scott's passion is infectious, and it didn't take him long to bring me round to his way of thinking. I can still recall where we sat and what we drank during our first conversation because it was such a remarkable turning point in my life. When he asked me to help him out, there was only one word that could come out of my mouth.

The Next Generation

My experience with Scott shows that you don't just have to pursue your own passion. You can get infected by other people's passion, as long as it aligns with what you think is important. In my case, I've been passionate about education throughout my entire life, and educating the next generation in particular.

That's true when it comes to the work I've been doing with Butterflies and Amandla, and it's also true when it comes to my support of the San Francisco Symphony and their attempts to bring in younger audiences through their teen nights. Classical music has been around for centuries, and not knowing anything

---

[29] "The Rice and Chessboard Legend," *Maths Careers,* April 26, 2021, https://www.mathscareers.org.uk/the-rice-and-chessboard-legend/

about it means that you're missing out in the same way as you're missing out if you don't know anything about literature or history.

It's like if you've never tasted herbs and spices. You could still get through life, and you could still eat, but you'd be missing out on a world of flavor. You'd be eating to live, without ever experiencing the joy that comes from living to eat.

Like I said in chapter one, children are our future. After all, they're the ones who will succeed us. If we want the world to be a decent place when we're no longer running it, we have to make sure that our children are properly educated. If nothing else, we need to do this for selfish reasons. Otherwise, we're not going to be able to live out our twilight years in peace and security.

That's the reason why I jumped at the chance to get involved with Butterflies and Amandla, although there are plenty of other opportunities out there. There are countless parts of the world where education is needed and where the kids need help. Some people help to prevent, treat, and cure diseases, while others help to fight poverty or provide clean water and proper sanitation.

Scapegoats

The key to turning passion into purpose is to find something that excites you and which aligns with your priorities in the world. When you're passionate about something, you'll find the time to do whatever needs to be done, even though you might think that you're fully occupied.

If you're going to spend that time doing something that drives you and makes you feel good about what you're doing, then you'll always find the time for it. If you're lucky and privileged enough to feel happy with the way in which you spend your time during the day, you'll sleep well at night and wake up the next morning feeling energized and wanting to do more.

The opposite is true too, which brings us back to those virtuous and vicious cycles. If you're upset when you go to bed, you're going to be restless for most of the night. You're going to worry about what went wrong and why it went wrong, and because you're only human, you're probably going to find yourself a scapegoat.

Unfortunately, we naturally tend to find someone else to blame for what went wrong, rather than accepting that we made a mistake. Once we start to do so, the vicious cycle begins, and there's no way out of it for the simple reason that you're blaming things on something that's beyond your control. You can't do anything to change it. You can only change yourself.

It may well be true that external factors are responsible for the problems that you're facing, but if that's really the case then it's a good idea to take a step back, to examine the situation and to see how you can make a change. If it's a job or a volunteering effort that's creating the problem, you might need to make a change and to find somewhere else where you can have a more positive impact.

Remember, you don't have to be the person who's going to change the world. You just have to be the person who's moving the needle towards the right direction. If you can help people to move beyond their limited set of circumstances—such as by introducing teens to classical music—you can open up the world for them.

Converting Passion into Purpose

Once you've explored what you're passionate about, the next step is to convert it into purpose. To do that, I find it useful to look for an organization that shares that passion and which works in an area which could help you to fulfill that passion. If you're interested in helping the unhoused in your community, look for an organization that works with people who don't have a place to stay.

When you've found an organization, you can go and volunteer to see what they're doing and where they need help. Most of these organizations have a range of volunteering opportunities available, and so you're sure to find something that works for you. Just because you don't know how to build a house, it doesn't mean that you can't help to solve the crisis of people not having homes to live in.

In the US, there's an organization called Habitat for Humanity which builds low-cost houses for people. Yes, they need people to build the houses, but they also need people to run the other parts of the organization. They need money to be able to buy the materials that are required to build a house, so you could help them to raise money. They need people to man the phones. They need people to find pieces of property that people are willing to sell and then to negotiate with them so that they can acquire it.

They also need people who are able to advocate on their behalf with the local authorities so that they can get permits more quickly and effectively. They need people to set up the services. You can't just build a house and expect people to live in it without plumbing, sewage systems, and fresh water. All this stuff requires expertise, and even if you don't have that expertise already, you can go ahead and acquire it.

Feel free to start slowly—work part-time, take on small projects, and dip your toes in to see if it's a good fit. Remember: if you think that you can't do something because you've never done it before, you'll never experience anything new.

There's a first time for everything; it's a cliché, but it's a cliché because it's true. Whether it's your first step, your first taste of a particular food, or your first time volunteering your services to help someone, you can't be afraid of taking that first step.

True, it's not always easy to take that step, which is why it's a good idea to start slowly. It's not a good idea to dive in and dedicate 100 percent of your time to something because you might not be able to follow through on it or you might find that it's not a good fit. There's nothing worse than committing yourself to doing something that you're no longer interested in doing.

On the other hand, if you take a first tentative step, you might decide to take another step because you know that the ground is firm beneath you. That's the key when it comes to turning your passion into purpose—the more you do something, the more it allows you to build on your passion and the easier it all becomes.

> ▷ **Action Item:** Revisit the action item from chapter four where we talked about the power of passion. Look for ways that you can take that passion and convert it into purpose. If you decide to do so by finding a charity to support, feel free to skip ahead to chapter eleven, where I've listed a number of fantastic organizations that are worthy of support.

Maslow's Hierarchy of Needs

I know a ton of people who are involved in all sorts of public service activities, but none of them started out by waking up one morning and saying, "I'm going to be a public servant." It's something that you walk your way into, and once you find something that excites you and fulfills you, you'll continue to do it.

The reason I stuck with volunteering for the alumni association was that I was getting as much back from it as I was putting into it. Sure, I was giving up my time to participate in the meetings, but they introduced me to a ton of incredible, interesting people. They're people who I now call my friends and who call me their friend.

The same is true of working with Butterflies and Amandla, both of which have enriched me in ways that are difficult to describe. That counts for a lot, because being purposeful about your passion isn't about getting a monetary reward. That's what you need to do for your day job to make sure that you have the monetary resources you need to feed and clothe your family.

You might have heard of Maslow's hierarchy of needs, a psychological framework created by Abraham Maslow which suggests that our human needs can be organized into a clear hierarchy, often depicted as a triangle or a pyramid. The idea is that our lower-level needs need to be satisfied before our higher ones.[30]

BiteSize Learning defines the five needs like so:[31]

1. Physiological needs (e.g. food, water, shelter, and rest)
2. Safety needs (e.g. security, stability, freedom from fear)
3. Social and belonging needs (e.g. friendship, intimacy, acceptance)
4. Esteem needs (e.g. respect, recognition, status)
5. Self-actualization needs (e.g. achieving your full potential, creativity)

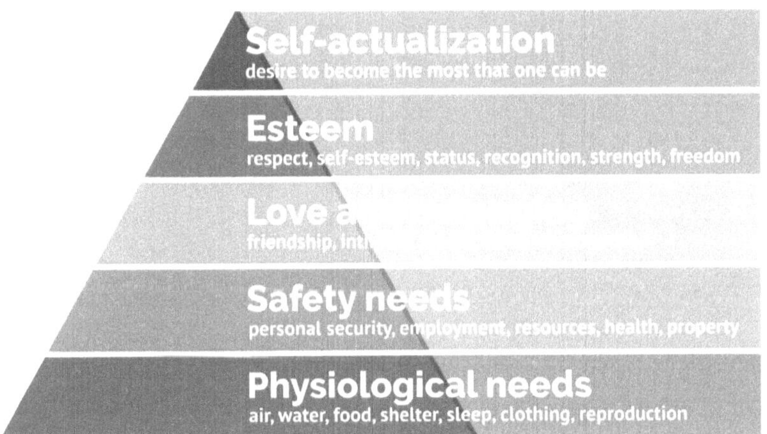

Maslow's hierarchy of needs

---

[30] Saul McLeod, PhD, "Maslow's Hierarchy of Needs," August 3, 2025, *Simply Psychology,* https://www.simplypsychology.org/maslow.html

[31] "Maslow's hierarchy of needs, explained," *BiteSize Learning,* https://www.bitesizelearning.co.uk/resources/maslows-hierarchy-of-needs-theory

Your day job helps you to take care of the bottom two or three layers of the hierarchy, while public service can help with the top three. It rewards you with a sense of fulfillment, of your purpose being achieved, of leaving the world a better place than you found it. There's a lot to be said for the peace of mind that comes from knowing that your children and your grandchildren are inheriting a planet that's fit for them to live in.

> ▷ **Action Item:** Study Maslow's hierarchy of needs and identify any layers that are currently unfulfilled in your own life. Now find ways to seek fulfilment, starting at the lowest unfulfilled layer and working your way up to the top.

The Power of Haircuts

Every six months or so, a hairdresser goes viral on social media for giving free haircuts to homeless people.[32] It's amazing how much of a difference it can make to someone if you give them a shave and a trim and help them to feel more presentable. It helps boost their self-confidence, while also ensuring that if they get the chance to interview for a job, they're better prepared to nail it.

It's also a great example of people converting passion into purpose. Their passion is hairdressing, and they cut people's hair during the week to pay the bills so that during the weekend, they can volunteer their time and turn their passion into purpose by helping those without a home.

When I visited the vets with my dogs during the COVID pandemic, the owners weren't allowed to go inside to help prevent disease transmission. The vets would come out to the car, collect the pet, call to explain what was going on, and then bring the pet back out.

---

[32] "Barber offers free haircuts to homeless people," video, *BBC News,* January 9, 2025, https://www.bbc.co.uk/news/videos/cwy38pp151vo

While I was waiting for them to finish up with my dogs, I saw a trailer across the way by the street. They had a couple of tables set up, some with clothes and others with toiletries, and people were going up and talking to them. It was pretty clear that those people were living on the streets because they were disheveled and unkempt.

It turns out that the trailer, run by an organization called Lava Mae, was a portable shower, and people could go up, take a shower, and pick up a change of clothes. By the time they came out, they'd undergone a transformation. They'd go in looking beaten down and depressed, barely walking upright, and they'd come out clean and holding their head up in the air.

The transformation was remarkable, and it was inspiring to see how the individuals responsible had turned their passion into purpose to solve a problem. They had to work with the city to get a permit so that they could park their trailer, connect to a fire hydrant to get water, and hook themselves up to the sewers so that the dirty water could be drained away. They'd done everything properly so that there'd be no chance of the police coming along and telling them to move on.

Finding Your Organization

If you can't find an organization (or you find one but you think they're not doing it right), the best thing to do is to create your own organization. That's exactly what Scott Clark was able to do in Cape Town. He visited South Africa while he was an undergraduate student, visited the shanty towns and saw a hole that needed to be filled. And so he decided to fill it.

If you have a particular passion you want to pursue and no other organization is tackling it or they're doing it in a way you don't agree with, why not start an organization of your own? It doesn't have to be big or to influence your entire community all at once. You can start by helping one person at a time; next week, you'll help two, then four, then eight.

You'll start talking to your friends about it, and you'll be so animated, excited, and enthusiastic that one or more of them will come along next week. Then they'll bring along some friends of their own. It becomes a virtuous cycle, and all of a sudden, it's not just you who's doing the work. You've got more people to help out, and the more people you have doing the work, the more people you can help.

If you're passionate about education, go to a school where the kids who graduate don't normally go to college. When that happens, part of the reason is usually because they think that college is for other people. If you finished college and are willing to spend your time volunteering at the school, you can show those kids that they're good enough to go to college.

Of course, being good enough to go to college is one thing and knowing how to do so is quite another. Remember, these kids are at a school where society has decided, "These kids aren't going to amount to anything and so we don't need to worry about them." They don't have counsellors and career advisors. They also don't have friends or family members who can tell them how to file an application.

Not everyone wants to go to college, and that's okay. It's all about providing them with opportunities if they decide they want to do so. If they don't, there are plenty of other ways to help. For example, I volunteered for a while at an organization that specialized in helping kids who'd decided not to go to college to develop their resumes. After all, most people don't know how to write a good resume. It's not a skill that we're born with.

I also worked with the kids to conduct mock interviews to teach them how to act if they were lucky enough to secure an interview. I showed them how to listen to and absorb questions and how to respond to them in a professional manner. They were amazed at how easy it all was and that they actually had it in them to have a career.

CHAPTER EIGHT

Overcoming Challenges

"The brick walls are there for a reason. They're not there to keep us out. The brick walls are there to give us a chance to show how badly we want something."

—Randy Pausch[33]

THE IDEA OF OVERCOMING CHALLENGES is universal. We all face challenges in life. In fact, you could argue that that's what life is all about. It's just a series of challenges for us to overcome, from when we first learn to walk and talk to when we're turning our passion into purpose and writing our legacies.

Interestingly enough, this isn't just true for humans—it's present everywhere, from marine life to land life and from animal life to plant life. It's all just a series of challenges. Take, for example, the plants that are growing in the rainforest and which can't get any sunlight because they're in the shadow of the giant trees growing all around them. They're constantly moving and adapting, trying to find that little spot where sunlight is filtered through the trees, because the trees keep sprouting new leaves and new branches and the spot that was sunny yesterday might not be sunny today.

That's what drives natural selection and evolution—the constant challenge between the hunter and the hunted. The hunter's challenge is that they need to be fast enough to catch its prey, while the hunted has the challenge of avoiding being captured. Maybe they can't run as fast as the hunter but they're nimbler or

---

[33] Brian Miller, "The Last Lecture, by Randy Pausch," *Brian T. Miller #DoGreatThings,* November 22, 2019, https://millerbrian.com/reading-log-2019/2019/12/3/the-last-lecture-by-randy-pausch

can climb trees. Natural selection will favor the animal that best adapts to meet its challenges… at least, until another challenge comes along.

When I first visited the Galápagos Islands back in 2017, I learned about an animal called the marine iguana. It turns out that marine iguanas evolved from land iguanas, which escaped from the mainland of South America and plunged into the ocean, where they gradually developed the ability to hold their breath over prolonged periods of time. Other than that, they're basically the same as the land iguana, except that they have different coloring because their camouflage adapted for life in the water, too. Marine iguanas are a greyish blue color that makes them blend into the water, while the land iguanas are sandy-colored or brown so that they can blend into the trees.

We don't credit iguanas with intelligence, but there was clearly some survival instinct at play that pushed them beyond what was "normal" for them. That's exactly how we humans can address a challenge.

The Scientific Method

When you come up against a challenge in your life—whether it's your personal, professional or volunteer life—one of the best ways to address it is to approach it like a scientist tackles a research problem. Of course, I'm a little biased because I'm a scientist and so I naturally tend to think that way, but I find that it's helpful in any situation.

One of the first things that you should do when you come up against an unexpected result or one that you didn't want or don't like is to examine what led to that result. When you look at it through the lens of it being a challenge that you're facing in your life or your career, you can examine what led up to that challenge in the first place. And when you examine what led up to the situation, it will often provide you with the solution as to how to fix or overcome it.

True, there will be times in life when you're up against something that's genuinely out of your control. When that's the case, you can't overcome that challenge by changing the inputs because those inputs are out of your control. If that happens, you may be better off practicing acceptance.

Whether you're religious or not, you might find it useful to remember the Serenity Prayer: "God, grant me the serenity to accept the things I cannot change, the courage to change the things I can, and the wisdom to know the difference."[34]

If the challenge came about because of something someone else did, you have an opportunity to talk to that person and have an open conversation about how they made you feel. This isn't about blaming them, because confrontations never solve anything, but rather about providing them with honest feedback in the hope that they'll decide to change their behavior.

This is a lesson that I learned the hard way back when I was working at the Lawrence Livermore National Laboratory. A technician that worked for me mustered the courage, after a great deal of soul searching and nervousness, to take me aside and give me feedback. He'd decided that the situation was bad enough that he had no other choice.

He said, "You're micromanaging us and not giving us ownership of what's happening in the lab. It's *our* lab, not *your* lab, and that's not the way it should be."

He was right, of course, but that didn't make it any easier for me to take his feedback on board. My first reaction was the same knee-jerk reaction that everyone else has. I thought that I couldn't possibly have been doing anything wrong because my bosses had been telling me that I was doing a good job. At the same

---

34 "The Serenity Prayer," *PrayWithMe.com*, accessed October 13, 2025, https://www.praywithme.com/serenity-prayer.html#google_vignette

time, it was true—I *was* micromanaging them. And that knee-jerk reaction wasn't going to help me to solve the problem.

Instead, I listened to them and made a change, and that worked out well for everyone. In my case, I became a better manager, while my employee was able to overcome an obstacle. He wouldn't have been able to do so if he hadn't approached the situation with the honesty and courage that he needed to address the situation.

If I'd been a different person, I might have turned round and said, "That's nothing to do with me. That sounds like it's your problem, not mine." I might have gotten annoyed for being put on the spot and it could have led to him suffering even more than he already was. But that's the risk you take in situations like this.

Even when there's a risk of it backfiring, I still think that the best way to address a challenge is to tackle it head-on, because when you do that, you either overcome the obstacle or you realize that you're going to have to deal with it differently. Either way, you shine a spotlight on the obstacle and make sure that you do something about it.

Every Challenge Is an Opportunity

When life throws a challenge your way, it's up to you how you respond to it. I find that it's useful to look at challenges as opportunities, because that's the most positive way of looking at things. There's a lot to be said for viewing the world as though your proverbial glass is half full, as opposed to half empty.

Like attracts like. If you act as though the glass is half empty, that's going to leave you predisposed to feel depressed. You'll think that you can't possibly solve the challenge you're dealing with. On the other hand, if you act as though the glass is half full, you feel like you're already halfway there. It seems as though you don't have as much work to do to reach the goal that you set out to attain.

That positive spin makes a huge difference—it's the secret sauce of successful people. They look at things more positively, and like attracts like. It becomes a virtuous cycle.

It also makes it more likely that they'll tackle a challenge head on, instead of leaving it unspoken and unresolved, which tends to eat away at you. It leads to a lot of bitterness and stops you from being happy. If the challenge is happening in the workplace, it's going to affect your performance because it's demotivating to feel unappreciated. You'll end up in a vicious cycle as opposed to a virtuous one.

True, the first time you encounter a challenge, it's perfectly fine to say, "Well, I'll give it another day." Perhaps you weren't thinking straight, or you didn't want to risk rushing into things because your emotions were running high. Thinking things through can also help you to be on your guard and to make sure that you don't overreact if the same situation presents itself in the future. That in itself can be a good thing.

There are circumstances in which a little reflection can solve a problem or prevent it from happening in the first place. Bear in mind that a lot of challenges take place because of misunderstandings, and that miscommunication is often at the root of that. We can misconstrue what's being said, in part because we view the world through a lens based upon the experiences we've had in the past. It's this that shapes the way that we address the challenges we come up against.

The "Aha" Moment

A challenge isn't something that you have to meet by yourself. There's help out there.

This is where having a mentor, a trusted circle of friends, or even a therapist can be super helpful. Talking things through with someone else gives you perspective—you start to see whether the problem you're facing is truly a challenge, and if so, what makes it one.

Two heads are better than one. When you talk through a problem, you sometimes realize that you've been blowing it out of proportion–and it isn't such a big deal. Better yet, you might come up with a solution.

As an aside, this is one of the reasons why I think it's useful to have people who are working in teams located at the same place. It's that accidental meeting in the hallway, by the water cooler, or at the coffee machine that gives you insights. Someone will ask you what's going on, you'll tell them, they'll ask you a follow-up question, and suddenly you'll think, "Aha! Now I know how to solve it."

When people work remotely, it's much more difficult to have those chance encounters. You could pick up the phone or send an email asking to arrange for a time to chat, but by the time you do that, it's become a structured conversation. The odds of having one of those moments of serendipity drop dramatically.

That's a problem, because most inspiration comes from those "Aha" moments, where something completely unrelated inspires you. For example, IKEA founder Ingvar Kampard experienced this when he couldn't fit a table in his car and decided to take its legs off. Jan Koum, the creator of WhatsApp, couldn't afford to call his father in Ukraine.[35] You generally don't get inspiration by sitting at a desk and beating your head against a computer screen.

Tackling the Bigger Challenges

Of course, some challenges are just too big for a single person to tackle. Just look at what Scott's doing with Amandla. Sure, one person could make a difference, but if you want to take on

---

[35] Brandon Gaille, "15 Famous Aha Moment Examples," *BrandonGaille.com*, February 1, 2015, https://brandongaille.com/15-famous-aha-moment-examples/

a bigger challenge—like servicing an entire shantytown—one person isn't going to be enough. You need a whole group to tackle those challenges.

Still, the same things apply whether you're tackling a challenge as an individual or whether you're doing it as part of a group. You still need to take the same kind of approach.

Collaboration is key to solving problems that are bigger than you because you're going to need help. With Amandla, Scott and his team can solve the problems in Philippi, but that's just one township outside one town. If you want to expand that to every child in South Africa (and who wouldn't?), you'll need more than one organization.

That's where collaboration comes in. By collaborating with other organizations that are working in other shanty towns throughout South Africa, Scott and his team can help them to hit the ground running.

In Butterflies' case, they're tackling bigger challenges with cooperative learning. What started out in Delhi as part of Butterflies' core program is now being rolled out elsewhere in India—not by setting up branches of Butterflies throughout the country, but by talking to educators and organizations who are pursuing similar missions in other states. We can teach them what's working for us in Delhi so that they can apply it to their own work.

Something similar happened to the children's Khazana, which has taken on a life of its own and even been adopted outside of India.

We've all heard of the butterfly effect—the idea that a single flap of a butterfly's wings can cause a tornado on the other side of the world—and it even gave me the title of the first chapter of this book. It's nice as a concept, but we often tend to oversimplify things.

The truth is that a single butterfly can't beat its wings and change the world. What it *can* do is that a beat of its wings can cause other butterflies to beat their wings, and that encourages other organisms to do other things, eventually leading to a chain reaction. It's that chain reaction that changes the world. The butterfly can't do it alone.

These bigger challenges are like a chain of challenges, with one leading into another. For example, if you're trying to buy a house then your overall challenge might be to buy the house, but there are a bunch of smaller challenges to tackle before then. You've got to find a property you like, make an offer that gets accepted and secure a mortgage. Once you've done all that, you've got to pack all your belongings, arrange the moving vans, and unpack everything after you move in.

These challenge chains are similar to what's happening with Butterflies and Amandla, but at a much bigger scale.

With Amandla, we're facing an even more existential challenge due to the shutting down of USAID, so now we're scrambling to raise significantly more money just to continue what we were already doing. That's a great example of a challenge that's caused by external factors. We've recognized that there's nothing we can do about that particular income stream, and so we've had to rethink the challenge. Rather than asking how we can reverse USAID's closure, we're now focusing on how to replace that funding altogether.

Like I said, overcoming obstacles is all about looking for ways to move forward, and when you can't move forward because an obstacle is in the way, you have to find your way around it.

Trying to convince USAID to keep giving us money would be like beating our heads against the proverbial brick wall. It wouldn't change anything; it would just give us headaches.

We know we can't go back in time and change things or recreate the agency, and so we're looking elsewhere. Again, it's a glass half full thing. A pessimist might think, "We're not getting funding anymore and so we're going to have to shut down." An optimist will look at it as an opportunity to diversify where the funding comes from.

This ties directly into the virtuous and vicious cycles we've talked about. If you approach a challenge with an optimistic point of view, it becomes much more possible. History is full of people who were "the first" simply because they refused to accept that something was impossible.

Whether you love him or hate him, Elon Musk provides some great examples of this. Tesla exists despite the fact that everyone said it wasn't possible to build a decent electric car. The same is true of SpaceX and its reusable rockets.

Speaking of rockets, the same idea applies to John F. Kennedy and his great proclamation that he intended to put a man on the moon before the decade was out. Like buying a house, that dream only became possible because it was broken down into smaller, tangible steps– achieving orbit, sending animals into space, then astronauts, and finally, the moon landing itself.

Even now, if we ever launch a manned mission to Mars and take Kennedy's vision a step further, that will only be possible because we first went to the moon. We'll probably build a base there and launch from its surface, because it's much easier to escape the moon's gravitational pull than it is here on earth.

That's another great example of how important it is to reframe challenges. In this case, instead of thinking about the huge amount of propulsion it would take to get from earth to Mars, we can launch from somewhere else.

Reframing the Challenge

Over time, you might find that the challenge you were originally trying to tackle is no longer relevant to where you want to be in life. Often, organizations get started because of a particular need at a particular time, and if all goes well, they get good at fulfilling that need and continue to do so.

The problem is that when everything is going well, most of us don't take a step back to examine where we are and what we're doing, along with whether doing it still makes sense. It's that whole idea of "if it ain't broke, don't fix it." We all have to deal with that, and it's a perfectly natural way of thinking, but sometimes a challenge can help you to refocus your thinking. If you're brave enough to take that step back, you might find that the real need today is different to what it was five, ten, or fifteen years ago.

When Greenpeace was first formed in 1970, it had the sole objective of stopping a nuclear weapons test in the Aleutians.[36] These days, that focus has changed and they're all about protecting the environment, because fewer nuclear weapon tests are taking place. The two things go hand-in-hand, but the organization has realized that its priorities need to shift with the times, which is why they've tackled everything from ocean litter to global warming. It also goes back to the title of the book and the need to pivot. It's not that they were doing the wrong thing—they were doing the right thing at the right time, but times have changed and so they've needed to realign themselves.

That's why, when you're working with a non-profit organization, it's useful to regularly reexamine whether your mission is still in line with the needs of the community you're serving, whether that's a group of children or an entire city. Don't waste your time trying to solve yesterday's problems if they no longer exist. With a bit of luck, you've done such a great job of tackling them that the problem just isn't there anymore.

---

[36] "Our history," *Greenpeace*, accessed October 13, 2025, https://www.greenpeace.org/usa/our-history.

Otherwise, it's like blindly following a satnav that's sending you down a road that leads into the ocean. Something similar happened to me back in 2022 when my wife and I met some friends in Ko Samui. There's a beautiful waterfall in the hills there and so we plugged the address into a GPS. The only problem was that the GPS was taking us to the top of the waterfall and not the bottom, which meant it was leading us through a forest we couldn't even pass through. Even if we'd made it to the other side, there was no point getting to the top of the waterfall when it can only be clearly seen and appreciated from the bottom.

We tried to follow the GPS three times because we were convinced that we'd made a mistake and that we weren't following it properly. Then one of us (not me) had the bright idea of asking a local.

Eventually, we *did* get to see the waterfall, but if we'd persisted with what we were doing, we would never have made it. There's a lesson there.

> ▷ **Action Item:** Take a step back and consider the challenges you face in your own life. Look for ways to reframe those challenges and, where possible, to turn them into opportunities. For the challenges that remain, make sure that tackling those challenges still makes sense and that you're not just pursuing outdated goals on autopilot.

Micro-Pivots

The message here is that if you want to overcome the challenges that come your way, you can't afford to let your doubts get in the way.

There's almost an epidemic of risk aversion. Just look at how many people say they have a great idea for a book but never actually write it. They know that the odds of success are stacked against them and so they never even try.

Anything new is inherently outside of our comfort zone, and so we tend to avoid it. The problem is that if we're unwilling to experience discomfort, we miss out on life's rich tapestry. Just look at food. If you go to a restaurant and see a dish that uses an ingredient you've never tried before, you might shy away from it, and then you'll never know whether you actually like it or not.

Just imagine if you'd done that with ice cream.

Perhaps this aversion to trying new things is ingrained in our hive mind because when we were living in caves, it was a bad idea to try going outside at night because you might not be able to come back. Fast forward to today, we don't want to try new foods or to experience new things unless we're backed by our friends and some sort of structure.

Fortunately, we've been gifted with the intelligence we need to understand that our fear of the unknown is just that—a fear. It isn't actually reality unless it manifests, which usually doesn't happen.

We see this happening all the time with business leaders who want to branch out and make a pivot. They've got a company with a product that's selling well, but they're afraid of taking the next step. They have to be willing to go outside their comfort zone because there's only so much they can do to improve their product, so what comes next? A different product or service, but only if they're brave enough to try something new.

If you give any business enough time, it's eventually going to reach a point at which the market is saturated, and you have as much market share as you're ever going to get. You need to break out of that, and that involves taking a risk. True, the launch might be a failure, but it also might unlock new or larger markets. It's a risk that's worth taking.

Risks are fundamental to every aspect of life. For example, if you want to make a new friend, you have to take the first step, which is to say hello. If the person in question doesn't respond well, you can move on, but at least you've learned something. The same is true if you want to ask someone out.

In my mind, not taking the risk is actually the riskier move. It can lead to stagnation, and there's also the risk that forces outside of your control will change the landscape and the path that you're on will suddenly be closed off or become redundant. We've seen that happen time and time again over the last few decades. Change is inevitable; you can't stop it.

Of course, I'm not suggesting taking outrageous risks just for the sake of it. Instead, it all comes back to dipping your toes into the water and taking little micro-pivots. The first change is usually the hardest. The second time is easier because you've done it before and you know it worked out in the end, even if there were some bumps along the way. By the time you've done it three or four times, it's no longer a big deal; it's just a normal course of action.

The goal should be that when a big catastrophe hits and everything changes, you can ride that change because you've already done it before.

My call-to-action here is for you to channel your fear into action. Let's say that you want to be a writer but you're afraid of taking the first step. Ancient Chinese philosopher Lao Tzu famously said, "A journey of a thousand miles begins with a single step."[37] When it comes to writing, a book of 300 pages begins with a single sentence.

Go ahead and write that first sentence. It doesn't matter whether it's good, because you'll have plenty of time to revisit it later on. The important thing is to start. It's amazing how quickly you can find your flow and overcome writer's block, whether you're a novice or a veteran.

---

[37] "Lao Tzu," *BBC World Service | Learning English | Moving Words*, accessed October 13, 2025, https://www.bbc.co.uk/worldservice/learningenglish/movingwords/shortlist/laotzu.shtml

To quote another aphorism that's commonly attributed to Henry Ford, "Whether you think you can or think you can't, you're right."[38] And so on that basis, why not think you can?

—————————

[38] quoteresearch, "Quote Origin: Whether You Believe You Can Do a Thing or Not, You Are Right," *Quote Investigator,* February 3, 2015, https://quoteinvestigator. com/2015/02/03/you-can/

PART FIVE

Legacy and Beyond

CHAPTER NINE

Writing Your Legacy

"In this world, nothing can be said to be certain, except death and taxes."

–Benjamin Franklin[39]

Legacy means different things to different people. For some, building a legacy is all about amassing a huge amount of wealth and passing it on to their heirs; for others, it has nothing to do with the amount of money you accumulate and instead is all about how you'll be remembered as a person. That starts with the people who are closest to you and then, as the circle expands, it includes more and more people who are further removed from you but whose life you've touched in one way or another.

I like to think of my legacy as being the way I'll be remembered. What would people say if they came to my memorial service? I'd like to be remembered for my actions–what I did to help people and how I made them feel, like Maya Angelou said in that quote at the start of chapter four. To me, that's what building a legacy is all about.

Every single one of us needs to decide what's important to us. It's never too late to start thinking about your legacy because there are only two things that are certain the moment you're born: death and taxes. And if we skip past taxes, we know that all of us will die and that most of us won't know when that's going to happen.

Not knowing when your life will come to an end means that you can't afford to wait until you reach some arbitrary age before you

---

[39] Madsen Pirie, "Death and Taxes," *Adam Smith Institute*, May 9, 2024, https://www.adamsmith.org/blog/death-and-taxes

start building your legacy. You have no guarantee that you'll actually make it to that age. Live your life as though you could die at any time, because you could.

A 55-year-old man has a one in 46,000 chance of dying on any given day, while a 55-year-old woman has a one in 79,000 chance. Driving a hundred miles on a motorcycle comes with a one in 26,000 chance of dying, while sky divers have a one in 101,000 chance of dying per jump.[40] These might sound like long odds, but they're nothing compared to the likelihood of you being born in the first place.[41]

Unless you're unlucky enough to have a fatal disease, you won't know when to expect the end and so you're better off living every day as if it were your last. If you *do* have a fatal disease, you're going to be too busy fighting the disease to think about your legacy. The only option is to start building your legacy before it's too late.

Writing your legacy is something you should think about and work towards every single day of your life. I find it helps to constantly ask yourself, "Am I doing things that make me happy and fulfill my passion?"

Of course, your passions might change as you grow, mature, and experience new things, and that's not necessarily a bad thing. You can't be passionate about something that you don't know exists. You have to experience things in order to know whether you're passionate about them.

---

[40] Spencer Greenberg, "Which Risks of Dying Are Worth Taking?," *Spencer Greenberg*, October 16, 2023, https://www.spencergreenberg.com/2013/10/which-risks-of-dying-are-worth-taking/
[41] Isabel Sepulveda, *"Odds of 50 random events happening to you,"* Stacker, March 29, 2025, https://stacker.com/stories/art-culture/odds-50-random-events-happening-you

The Search for Fulfillment

The search for fulfillment and the quest to build your legacy needs to take place simultaneously as you work on your career. Keep an eye on whether what you're doing is fulfilling or not. If you find that it's not satisfying you at a level that makes you happier and therefore a better person to be around, it's time to think about making a change.

If you're driven to build the next big thing—and to make a ton of money in the process—then that's perfectly fine. That's your legacy and you should pursue it. Even then, if you're pursuing a particular area but you feel more passionate about another piece of technology that excites you more, perhaps you should think of making that pivot.

In my case, I was quite happy as a scientist, helping the world to get to the point where nuclear fusion becomes a commercial reality and grants us the ability to access unlimited electrical power for very little money and without the deleterious effects of burning fossil fuels or running a conventional reactor. That was fulfilling for a certain amount of time, but after that, it was no longer enough. I realized that I wasn't going to be able to achieve as much as I wanted to.

That's when I first decided to make a pivot, which started with me taking a few baby steps while continuing to work in the profession that I'd chosen for myself. In fact, even with all of the charitable work that I do today, I'm still happily involved with the field.

My pivot didn't come because I was frustrated with what I was doing, unchallenged, unhappy, or underpaid. I just felt that I wasn't able to help enough people or to make as much of an impact on the world as I wanted to. I wasn't leaving people better for having interacted with me.

That's a very personal goal that's grounded in my own passions and my search for fulfillment. You have to determine your own goals and build your legacy for your own reasons.

If you're stuck in a rut, it's a good idea to make a change. If that means you're going to pivot into public service, get involved with non-profits, or help local communities, that's great. But if that means you're going into a different line of work but continue working in the for-profit arena, that's fine too.

At the end of the day, legacy is about how people will remember you. If you're unhappy with what you're doing, you're not going to make a positive impact. You're going to be unhappy and grumpy, which will lead you back into the vicious cycle we talked about, which will only make things worse. People will start avoiding you because they wouldn't want to interact with someone who isn't pleasant to be around, and the cycle will go on and on.

The Link Between Mind and Body

Building the legacy you want requires a concerted effort of self-reflection—taking the time to look at what you're doing and asking whether you're spending your time where it matters most. I tend to do that while I exercise, because if I'm already exercising my body and working to become stronger physically, it makes sense to simultaneously work on becoming stronger mentally and spiritually.

As a species, we've done a lot of work to figure out the physical side of our beings. We know a lot about diagnosing, preventing and treating diseases, and while we still have plenty of work to do, we've made a lot of progress. When it comes to our minds, though, we're a lot further behind. Even though we've made some significant advances, there's a lot of work left to do before we understand the mind as much as the body.

The same is true when it comes to our approach to mental and physical wellbeing. When someone has a physical illness, everyone looks at them and recognizes that they're suffering and that they need assistance. When they have a mental illness, people turn to them and say, "What's wrong with you? Fix yourself." But that's not a helpful way of looking at things.

True, we've made a lot of progress in recent years, but we also have a long way to go. We all know to seek help from a doctor when we have a physical issue, but not everyone knows how to do that for the mental and spiritual side of things, which are equally important.

That's highlighted by the fact that in today's workplace, it's acceptable to call in physically sick but it's still stigmatized to take a sick day if you're struggling with your mental health. That's super short-sighted, because it's counterproductive to force people to go to work. It's not going to be good for them, and it's not going to be good for their coworkers. When someone's having a bad day, it makes everything worse for everyone around them.

We recognize that if someone's suffering from a virus, it's not a good idea for them to go into the office because they'll infect everybody else and the whole team is going to suffer. What we don't realize is that the same is true if you're struggling with your mental health. If you feel like you can't take a mental health day, you'll go into the office and end up saying or doing things that upset other people, which will make them have a bad day as well. It's another negative spiral, and if you're not careful, you'll drag everyone down with you.

We need to start thinking of mental health issues being as contagious as physical illnesses. Let's face it, it's only since the COVID pandemic that it's become acceptable to say, "I have a cold and so I'm going to work from home." Before that, most people would go into the office anyway, and then they'd spread bacteria around and everyone else would get sick. The cold would spread around the office, and people would take it home and infect their families. The downward spiral would continue.

In fact, the common cold costs US businesses $25 billion per year, with two-thirds of that from lost job productivity.[42] Meanwhile, it's estimated that unplanned absences due to poor mental health costs the economy $47.6 billion per year.[43] We're oversimplifying here, but there's an argument to be made that mental health struggles are twice as common as the common cold.

Passion and Purpose Revisited

We've already talked about turning passion into purpose, and so now it's time for us to take things to the next step. That can be done by using purpose to build your legacy—although we should also note that passion and purpose can change.

For example, a lot of celebrities say that they always wanted to be rich and famous and then once they actually became rich and famous, they realized that it wasn't solving any of their problems. True, they might have a better quality of life and more disposable income, but they still have the same problems that they had before. That's when they realize that fame and fortune isn't all that it's cracked up to be and that something is missing.

This can lead to either a positive or negative. When it's positive, people find new purposes and are empowered to pursue them because they don't have to worry about paying their rent. They can focus on building their legacy. When it's negative… well, that's why it's not uncommon for them to turn to drink or drugs.

---

[42] Alexa Lardieri, "Cost of a common cold: Study reveals how expensive it is to come down with seasonal bugs in 152," *Mail Online*, November 26, 2023, https://www.dailymail.co.uk/health/article-12772579/Cost-common-cold-Study-reveals-expensive-come-seasonal-bugs-152-countries.html
[43] Dan Witters and Sangeeta Agrawal, "The Economic Cost of Poor Employee Mental Health," *Gallup.com*, November 2, 2022, https://www.gallup.com/workplace/404174/economic-cost-poor-employee-mental-health.aspx

When it comes to that positive cycle, you hear about actors and actresses who quit acting because they decided that raising their family was more important than fame and fortune. Rock stars decide that they don't want to go on tours anymore because they can't have much of a family when they're on the road for 200 days a year.

Of course, putting family life on hold to pursue a rock star career is fine if that's what you want and you're making a conscious decision to do so. There's also the fact that our priorities can change. People often don't realize where their priorities really lie until they have a family. It's that classic thing where you don't know what you've got until it's gone, and you don't know what you haven't got until you've got it.

That's why a lot of people reach middle age and suddenly realize they're not as young as they used to be. They decide it's time to get in shape—not just to live longer, but to actually enjoy the years they have left instead of progressively more unfit. An ounce of prevention, as the saying goes, is worth far more than a pound of cure.

Also, it's not about the quantity of years that you have—it's about the quality. Your health span is just as important as your lifespan, if not more so. That's why it's so important to eat well and stay in shape so that you can avoid things like heart disease and diabetes. Even if you have a health condition that doesn't shorten your life, it can affect its quality.

Even if you have a rare disease that means you're not going to live past forty, you should make sure that you can enjoy those years as much as possible. Maybe that way, you won't have to spend your final years in a home, and you'll also give yourself the best possible chance of building your legacy.

One of the problems with our society is that when an issue affects people's quality of life, we don't see it as urgent. If you're trying to cure cancer, there'll be no shortage of people who are willing to help, whether that's by donating their money or their expertise. But if you're working to cure osteoporosis or arthritis, it's a lot harder to get people involved. These conditions don't kill, but they can make life so difficult that people feel as though they might as well. They might live on, but often in pain or frustration for the last ten, fifteen, or twenty years of their life.

Putting Things Into Perspective

There's an argument to be made, thanks to the internet, that everyone will live forever because the things that they've posted online will stick around long after they've gone. British Comic fantasy novelist Terry Pratchett, who we'll hear from at the start of chapter eleven, put it best when he wrote, "Do you not know that a man is not dead while his name is still spoken?"[44]

That's true whether you're Mahatma Gandhi, John F. Kennedy, or Joe Shmoe, remembered only by your friends and family. It also puts things into perspective—a reminder that none of this is going to matter in a million years anyway. There won't be anyone left to speak our names.

With the way we're going at the moment, with global warming and the constant threat of World War III, it might be a lot less than a million years.

I'd like to finish this chapter with a nod to the classic epiphanies we see in *A Christmas Carol* and *A Wonderful Life*. When Scrooge gets visited by the ghosts of Christmas Past, Present, and Future, he realizes that people won't remember him for the money he's accumulated. They'll remember him for the way he made them feel, like Maya Angelou said, and that's what led to his decision to change his ways before it was too late.

A Wonderful Life approaches things from a different direction, looking back after the protagonist's death at the difference his

---

[44] Terry Pratchett, *Going Postal* (Doubleday, 2004).

life made and asking whether the world would have been a better place if he'd never lived. Interestingly, *A Wonderful Life* is based on Philip Van Doren Stern's *The Greatest Gift*, which itself is inspired by *A Christmas Carol*.[45]

A Christmas Carol and *A Wonderful Life* are both great stories, but these moments of epiphany don't happen in the real world. None of us is going to be visited by the ghosts of Christmas Past, Present, and Future, and we're certainly not getting a chance to look back at our lives after we pass away. Instead, we need to make those decisions now. We have to be our own ghosts.

Remember that the legacy you build is up to you. If accumulating a vast amount of wealth is what moves you, that's okay. Today, Scrooge is a byword for a mean, miserly person who spends as little money as possible, but we shouldn't ignore the fact that you can pursue wealth and be a good person at the same time.[46]

It's true that Scrooge was an unpleasant person, but he didn't have to be. In fact, what we don't see after the end of *A Christmas Carol* is that even after his change of heart, Scrooge probably continued to make money and to be successful in business. The difference is that to begin with, he was accumulating money at the expense of all else. By the end of the novel, he's realized that there's more to life than wealth.

Besides, accumulating money can make a lot of sense if you're doing it to take care of your family, especially if you have a ton of kids and you want them to have a better life than you did. And after all, why wouldn't you want that? Your goal as a parent should always be to make sure that your kids have a better life than you.

So many older people complain that today's kids have things too easy compared to when they were young. Isn't that the point? If

---

[45] American Film Institute, *"It's a Wonderful Life,"* *AFI Catalog*, accessed October 14, 2025, https://catalog.afi.com/Catalog/moviedetails/27682

[46] "Scrooge," *Collins English Dictionary*, 2025, https://www.collinsdictionary.com/dictionary/english/scrooge

today's kids still have to do all the hard stuff we had to do when we were young, we've let them down.

When you've been in a position where you had to suffer, you don't want that to happen to your kids—or, by extension, to any kids. That's why I do what I do in the first place.

And that also brings me back to my own story.

CHAPTER TEN

Childhood Trauma

"Turn your wounds into wisdom."

—Oprah Winfrey

WHEN I WAS A CHILD, I experienced some childhood trauma which had a huge impact on my life and is a big reason why I'm the person I've become.

In December 2020, when the world was in lockdown due to COVID-19, my mother passed away in India. I'd last visited her just before the lockdowns in March 2020—we scooted out just in time and they pretty much slammed the doors shut behind us as we returned. The day before she passed, she called me while I was on a paddleboat with my wife and kept telling me over and over again, "I'm so sorry for what happened when you were a child."

At the time, I had no memory of the trauma that I went through, and so I couldn't understand what she meant and didn't think about it too much.

Meanwhile, my brother, who lives in England, went out to New Delhi to help my father. A couple of days after he arrived, he called me to say, "We found Ma's will, and before I send it over to you, I want you to know that I had absolutely nothing to do with it."

Yet again, I couldn't understand what he was talking about—that is, until he sent me photos of the will, which said that she'd left every-thing to my brother, including the responsibility of caring for my father. That was a big surprise, because even though I lived 9,000 miles away, I used to make two or three trips a year to visit them and to help out and make sure they were okay. They used to call me at odd hours throughout the day, and I'd help them out with whatever tech problems they were having.

While I was still reeling from all of this, my mother-in-law developed lymphomatic cancer. Fortunately, her son was out in India with her and so there was no immediate need for us to go, but my wife was keen to go out there as soon as possible. Her mother was almost 90 years old and had been very clear that she didn't want to be treated for the cancer. She wanted to go standing up, instead of being confined to her bed for months on end and dependent upon an army of carers.

She got her wish, too. When she finally passed, she'd only been bed-bound for a couple of days. When my time is up, I hope that's how I go, too.

My mind had continued to turn while my wife was away. We were in lockdown, and I had a lot of time to think. When my wife came home early February 2021, she wore protective gear around me—we were both worried about COVID. I was cooking dinner, making steak. She said something, I replied, and then all of a sudden, all of the puzzle pieces clicked into place. A repressed memory from my childhood surfaced.

I couldn't help it. I suddenly blurted out, "My father sexually abused me when I was a child."

The Memories Return

When I told her that, my wife took off her protective gear and wrapped me up in a huge hug. She told me, "I don't care if we get COVID. If we die, we die together."

After that, more and more memories started coming back to me. It hadn't just happened once or twice; it happened repeatedly over a period of several years, starting when I was a pre-teen. I felt as though I'd done something wrong—that it was my fault and that I'd somehow created the situation.

All of a sudden, everything was clear to me. I understood why my mother had cut me out of the will and why she'd been mean to me throughout my teenager years. She'd looked at me as someone who was taking her husband's affection away from her.

Let's not forget that we're looking back at this from the 21ˢᵗ century, where things like this are much more of an open problem. We know that both boys and girls get abused, often by people in positions of power over them, whether that's a parent, an uncle, a minister, a priest, or a teacher. It's rampant and it's everywhere.

Back when it was happening to me in the 1970s, I had absolutely no one I could turn to. I knew full well that if I told anyone, they wouldn't believe me. My father was a respected civil servant, high up in the Indian government. They'd say, "You're wrong, he can't be doing something like that. Someone is making you tell stories."

In fact, even if you fast forward to today, my brother still doesn't believe me. So in retrospect, it looks like I was absolutely right not to tell anyone.

The whole thing left me absolutely convinced that I wasn't lovable and that nobody would ever be able to love me because of the terrible sin I'd committed. That's what pushed me into being a loner and not wanting to interact with other people. I thought that the more I talked to people, went out, and had fun, the more likely I was to slip up and give up my secret—and then people would see me as evil and want nothing to do with me.

Looking back, I know I was wrong. It also helped that I found the strength to talk to one of my dear childhood friends about it all. She was very supportive. She said, "I wish I'd known. I wish you'd told me."

I told her how I'd felt, and she replied, "I understand that's how you felt, but I can tell you honestly that if you'd told me, I would have supported and believed you."

The problem is, hindsight is always 20/20, and there's no way for me to go back and redo the experiment and to see what might have happened if I'd done things differently. That's just life. We haven't figured out time travel yet.

How Our Youth Informs Our Adulthood

Even though I'd completely shut all of this out of my memory, it still had a huge impact on the way I behaved as an adult. When I met my wife and first felt attracted to her, I thought I couldn't afford to tell her what had happened. I was convinced that if I did, she'd run a mile, because I was damaged goods and an evil person. She's the best thing that's ever happened to me, and I wanted to avoid doing anything that might jeopardize our relationship. And so I worked even harder to suppress the memories.

Part of the reason why I got into photography was because, as a child, it was something I could do alone. I got into developing my own photos so that I could isolate myself from the rest of humanity and be alone in the dark room. I didn't have to worry about what other people thought of me or whether I'd reveal my secret. Photography became both a refuge and a form of therapy, helping me recover from trauma and other unfortunate situations.

The other thing that happened is that I developed an affinity for children which I didn't quite understand. In particular, I felt a huge amount of empathy for children who found themselves in awful circumstances through no fault of their own.

Back in 2012, I was picked as a juror for a civil case involving a young woman who accused her minister of abusing her when she was a child and getting her pregnant. She'd been forced to file the civil case after the criminal one was dismissed for lack of evidence, which happens a lot.

When she took a stand and began to speak, I immediately understood what she'd been through. I didn't know why at the time, but

I believed her completely. I knew she was telling the truth. We eventually found the defendant guilty and liable for damages.

As everyone was leaving the jury room, she came up to me and said, "I want to thank you personally." I asked her what for, and she said, "Because I was looking at you throughout the trial, and I could tell that there was at least one person in that courtroom who understood what I was feeling." There must have been something in my facial expression or my body language that made it clear that showed her I empathized. She didn't say it outright, but I suspect she somehow knew that something similar had happened to me.

Now that all of this is out of my repressed memory and into my real, actual memory, I find that I can see these things happening. When I'm thinking in a certain way, I know why that is. It's because of what's happened to me.

By now, I've told just about everyone I know. I've had therapy to help me to come to terms with what happened, and I even talked to my father about it–sort of. I didn't have a conversation with him, but I sent him a text message. His response was both startling and very telling. He said, "That happened so long ago. Why are you bringing it up now? I loved your mother very much, you know."

I'm sure he did, but what did that have to do with anything?

Still, it was at least a form of confirmation. It proved to me that I wasn't hallucinating and that I hadn't imagined it. That's also backed by all of the different memories I have. It used to happen when we went out for dinner. My father would have a beer or a whiskey or two, and when we got home, he'd open another–and hand one to me. The abuse would start after that.

It reached a point where I couldn't eat certain types of food because they reminded me of the restaurant that we used to go to, though I couldn't explain why. I was okay with it when it was cooked at home, but I couldn't eat it in a restaurant because it reminded me of those dark days in my childhood, which I'd worked so hard to forget.

It was only when the memory popped out that I understood it all. My therapist told me that's not unusual when it comes to abuse cases and that it's a common coping mechanism. People often try to repress and bottle up their memories, but then they pop back at unexpected times because they're all still there, sitting just below the surface. It's not possible to erase them.

You can't erase trauma; you can only learn to deal with it. You can overcome it, but it can never be erased because you can't go back in time and stop it from happening. You can't re-do your life. None of us get do-overs.

Abuse and Trauma

The abuse that I suffered has been a pivotal part of my journey as a human being, and it's why I don't want anyone to suffer the way that I did, because I suffered in ways that are unimaginable to anyone who hasn't been through something similar.

The person I'd trusted the most was the one who betrayed me, and I was furious with my father for a number of years because of it. My mother said that I was a horrible teenager because I couldn't stand being in the same room as him. We were constantly at loggerheads, and I refused to talk to him. I didn't want him to feel that I enjoyed his company in any sense, because I was terrified that I'd accidentally encourage him.

Let's not forget that I was completely powerless. I thought about telling people, especially my aunt, but I was worried that nobody would believe me. My mother certainly wouldn't have, and neither would my grandparents or any of the other elders. I could have said something at school, but back in those days, teachers didn't usually act on things like that.

It was the seventies, and life was very different then. Today, we're in a completely different era where we've learned to have greater awareness about all these issues. If a child reports something like that now, the teacher is duty-bound to act on it. They have protocols in place that say exactly what they have to do, and they're trained to make sure that the kids are safe. They know it has to be reported up the chain and that it has to be passed onto a qualified professional who has the tools and the training to know how best to support the child.

Now, it could be that the abuse didn't actually take place. I don't believe that every child that says they've been abused actually has been. Sometimes, there are misunderstandings. A child might hear about another child's experience and begin to believe something similar happened to them. It's possible, though it isn't exactly common.

At the same time, children are becoming more empowered to speak up, in the same way that women have been empowered through movements such as #MeToo. This is true for all forms of abuse, not just sexual. Mental and physical abuse can be just as bad, though I'd say that it's easier to recover from a physical injury than a mental one. Part of that is because we understand the body so much better than the mind. We can replace limbs and organs, perform transplants, even rebuild parts of the body—but the mind remains far more mysterious.

While writing this chapter, I started revisiting one of my favorite jazz musicians from childhood, Chuck Mangione, who passed away in July 2025.[47] In particular, I couldn't stop listening to *Children of Sanchez*—the soundtrack to the 1978 film of the same name, which won Mangione a Grammy for Best Pop Instrumental Performance. I can distinctly remember listening to it for the first time when I was in college.

---

[47] Evan Bourtis, "Rochester music legend Chuck Mangione has died at age 84," *News10NBC*, July 25, 2025, https://www.whec.com/top-news/rochester-music-legend-chuck-mangione-has-died-at-age-84/

That song helped me through some tough times and remains one of the main inspirations behind my desire to help children. One section in particular stands out to me: *"Every child belongs to mankind's family. Children are the fruit of all humanity. Let them feel the love of all the human race."*[48]

I was introduced to Mangione by a friend of mine who was a huge fan of jazz music. I hadn't heard anything like it before, and I quickly fell in love with the sound of the trumpet and the flugelhorn. I find that there's something both melodic and haunting about a trumpet that's played well. It's like a violin in that it seems to offer a quick connection to human feelings that few other instruments are able to do.

I think that's because it doesn't have the plucking sound of other stringed instruments, which separates each note from the next. The notes tend to blend in with one another, and there's something about that which catches my imagination and links directly to my psyche.

Wind instruments are powered by breathing, which is the most human thing there is. Playing the guitar or piano requires you to use your hands, like using a tool, while wind instruments can be as primal as whistling or singing.

Some of the most haunting and powerful pieces of music ever written are performed by the human voice. You don't even have to speak the language. A lot of classical music is in Italian, French, or German, but you can still get a good sense of what's being communicated even if you can't speak the language. We still see that happening today with K-pop, which has a musical export value of over $1 billion.[49] It can move people whether or not they

---

48 "Chuck Mangione (Ft. Don Potter) – Children of Sanchez (Overture) Lyrics," *Genius*, accessed October 14, 2025, https://genius.com/Chuck-mangione-children-of-sanchez-overture-lyrics

49 Statista Research Department, "Music industry in South Korea - statistics & facts," *Statista*, April 17, 2025, https://www.statista.com/topics/5098/music-industry-in-south-korea/

can speak Korean, and in many ways, it breaks language barriers and brings people together.

Getting back to my rediscovery of Chuck Mangione, I wanted to mention him here because those lyrics that I quoted could well be about the work that I do with Amandla and Butterflies, which is all about tackling the suffering of children. Like I said, that suffering doesn't have to take the form of sexual or physical abuse. A big part of what we do is to tackle the trauma that comes from not knowing whether you're going to be able to eat.

Escaping the Past

You can't escape your past or the circumstances in which you came into this world.

There are people out there who've had privileged upbringings and who've been given everything they ever wanted. They're privately educated and get straight to the top of their fields because their parents knew people, and they had everything handed to them. Some people rebel against that. They end up in a downward spiral because they don't *want* to have everything handed to them.

That reminds me of the story of Hildegart Carballeira, who was conceived and raised as an experiment by her mother, Aurora. Aurora Carballeira was a eugenicist and staunch feminist who aimed to raise her daughter to be the woman of the future. Hildegart spoke four languages when she was eight and finished law school as a teenager. But unfortunately, she never made it to her 20th birthday.

As cultural journalist Juan Carlos Saloz explains, "The more Hildegart stood out, the more jealous her mother became. Hildegart was starting to think for herself, to make her own decisions. She wanted to explore the world, distance herself from her mother's rigid plans, and fly with her own wings. And this, for

Aurora, was a betrayal. After many push and pull moments in an exceptional love-hate relationship, Aurora took a gun one early morning in June 1933 and entered her daughter's room while she slept. She shot her four times and ended her life when she was only 18 years old."[50]

Aurora's story is a great example that if you try to over-coach somebody or force them to do what you want them to do, rather than what they want to do, it's not going to work.

A bit part of what Butterflies and Amandla do is to provide kids with the opportunities and infrastructure they need to discover things for themselves. The kid who wanted to be the bank manager is a great example of that. He didn't do that because his parents told him that he had to—he did it because it was something that he discovered by himself.

---

[50] Juan Carlos Saloz, "The true story behind Hildegart Rodríguez, the fascinating protagonist of The Red Virgin," *Softonic*, September 23, 2024, https://en.softonic. com/articles/the-true-story-behind-hildegart-rodriguez-the-fascinating-protagonist-of-the-red-virgin

PART SIX

A Call to Action

CHAPTER ELEVEN

Join the Movement

"No one is finally dead until the ripples they cause in the world die away."

—Terry Pratchett, *Reaper Man*

IF MY LIFE STORY has inspired you to do something, to help to drive change in the world, I ask you to come and join me.

There are countless different ways you can add value to the world. You could concentrate on doing what you're doing now to the best level you possibly can. You could focus on being the best person you can possibly be. And you could join organizations like the two that I support to try and make the world a better place.

If you'd like to support the causes that I've been involved with, there are many ways you can help. The simplest way is to give money, because that's always a primary, urgent need for any organization that's trying to work in the developing world.

You can find more information about them by visiting their websites, which are listed below:

- Amandla: www.amandladevelopment.org
- Butterflies: www.butterfliesusa.org

If you're interested in doing more, we'd love for you to pay us a visit. Go to New Delhi or to Cape Town and be inspired, as I was when I visited them myself. You could also consider joining us by becoming a member of the board, contributing your time and talent in addition to, or instead of, your money.

If you have any particular skillsets that you're interested in offering to an organization like the two that I support, that's also super helpful. In the US, we're all volunteers and we don't hire anyone. We do that deliberately because we want to give as much of the money we raise as possible to the organizations that are working with the kids on the front line. The only costs that we have in the US are minor costs related to running the website. Almost every dollar that people give goes to the local organizations.

And if you're inspired but you want to do something different, I call for you to do that as well.

Children's Organizations

If I've inspired you to want to help with children's organizations, there are plenty of them around the US, as well as elsewhere in the world. I'd recommend starting with UNICEF, because you can either work directly with them or you can use them as a resource to find other organizations in other parts of the world that might be of greater interest to you.

Here's a list of children's organizations that I'd recommend (mind you, there are many others too), starting with UNICEF:

- UNICEF (United Nations Children's Fund): www.unicef.org
- Save the Children: www.savethechildren.org
- World Vision: www.worldvision.org
- Plan International: www.plan-international.org
- SOS Children's Villages: www.sos-childrensvillages.org
- Compassion International: www.compassion.com
- ChildFund International: www.childfund.org
- Room to Read: www.roomtoread.org
- Children International: www.children.org
- The Global Fund for Children: www.globalfundforchildren.org

Other Ways to Help People

If working with children isn't your thing, there are plenty of other areas with a huge amount of need. For example, there are organizations that focus on preventing diseases from spreading, such as Doctors Without Borders.

Meanwhile, due to the wars that are raging around the globe, there are millions of displaced people who need urgent assistance, particularly due to the US government reducing the amount of money that's being spent on aid programs. It would be super helpful if you could help to pick up some of the slack.

Here are a few organizations that work to help refugees and displaced people:

- Doctors Without Borders: www.doctorswithoutborders.org
- UNHCR (United Nations High Commissioner for Refugees): www.unhcr.org
- International Rescue Committee (IRC): www.rescue.org
- Refugees International: www.refugeesinternational.org
- Norwegian Refugee Council: www.nrc.org
- International Organization for Migration (IOM): www.iom.int
- Hebrew Immigrant Aid Society (HIAS): www.hias.org
- Jesuit Refugee Service (HRS): www.jrs.net
- Mercy Corps: www.mercycorps.org
- Relief International: www.ri.org

If education inspires you, there are organizations that go to areas where students from middle school and high school don't typically realize that college education is within their reach.

There's financial aid on offer for colleges around the country, and students in underprivileged areas with parents who didn't go to college themselves often don't know that financial aid is available.

It's true that certain colleges are out of reach of people who aren't extremely wealthy or who can't take out large sums of money as a loan. There are plenty of programs out there available to people with little to no means of their own.

You can work with organizations like the following:

- QuestBridge: www.questbridge.org
- The Posse Foundation: www.possefoundations.org
- College Possible: www.collegepossible.org
- Bottom Line: www.bottomline.org
- College Track: www.collegetrack.org
- uAspire: www.uaspire.org
- ScholarMatch: www.scholarmatch.org
- Center for First-Generation Student Success: www.imfirst.org
- Breakthrough Collaborative: www.breakthroughcollaborative.org
- College Bound: www.collegebound.org

Throughout my life, I've learned that education is of primary importance. It's a way to move up in the world, to change your circumstances, and to write your own legacy. Because of that, I'd encourage every young person who isn't yet college educated to go out and get an education if they feel like that's the right decision for them.

I wouldn't say that everyone should get a college education, because that's not necessarily the case. I just want to make sure that people who are interested in getting a college education are able to pursue that, even if they think that they can't afford to do so.

Sometimes, college isn't right for someone because of what they want to do in life, but there are other options like apprenticeships and on-the-job training. If you want to be a mechanic and to work on cars, you might not need a college degree, but there are programs out there where you can get a job and learn while you're working.

There are vocational programs and apprenticeship programs where you can master a trade. For example, in the US, there's a shortage of plumbers and electricians, and so if you're good with your hands and you want to get into either of those fields, you don't need a college degree. You can just apprentice yourself to a master in the trade. You'll make good money and have a fulfilling life, and you won't have to carry any kind of debt.

Another thing to consider getting involved in is protecting the environment, both locally and throughout the globe as a whole. There are lots of ways to do just that, and there are plenty of companies that are developing green technologies or making sustainability affordable. When you're in a position of comfort and you're able to afford things, it's easy to say that people shouldn't buy things that aren't sustainable as opposed to the cheaper version that's going to pollute the environment. But not everyone can afford to pay the added markup for a product that's made sustainably.

Here are some environmental organizations that you might be interested in supporting:

- Natural Resources Defense Council (NRDC): www.nrdc.org
- Sierra Club: www.sierraclub.org
- Environmental Defense Fund (EDF): www.edf.org
- The Nature Conservancy: www.nature.org
- Earthjustice: www.earthjustice.org
- Friends of the Earth US: www.foe.org
- 350.org: www.350.org
- Greenpeace: www.greenpeace.org
- Center for Biological Diversity: www.biologicaldiversity.org
- Climate Reality Project: www.climaterealityproject.org

We also talked about supporting people who are homeless, and there are plenty of organizations that help people to survive and find shelter. Some of those include:

- National Alliance to End Homelessness: www.endhomelessness.org
- Coalition for the Homeless: www.coalitionforthehomeless.org
- Shelter Partnership: www.shelterpartnership.org
- The Salvation Army USA: www.salvationarmyusa.org
- Covenant House: www.covenanthouse.org
- Housing Works: www.housingworks.org
- Project HOME: www.projecthome.org
- Back On My Feet: www.backonmyfeet.org
- People Assisting the Homeless (PATH): www.epath.org
- National Coalition for the Homeless (NCH): www.nationalhomeless.org

I talked about how I'm a passionate supporter of the San Francisco Symphony, and there are a number of organizations out there who help to support classical music. You can help to support organizations like these:

- League of American Orchestras: www.americanorchestras.org
- Chamber Music America (CMA): www.chambermusicamerica.org
- Classical Music Rising: www.classicalmusicrising.org
- American Composers Forum: www.composersforum.org
- Sphinx Organization: www.sphinxmusic.org
- From the Top: www.fromthetop.org
- National Association for Music Education (NAfME): www.nafme.org
- Opera America: www.operaamerica.org
- American Musicological Society: www.amsmusicology.org
- Music Teachers National Association (MTNA): www.mtna.org

There are also plenty of organizations that are helping to combat food poverty. For example, some of them create urban farms so that people don't have to buy product from grocery stores where they're flying it in from the other side of the world. We create an awful lot of pollution just to be able to buy strawberries out of season.

Meanwhile, in the United States, 47 million people are food insecure, and that includes 14 million children. In 2023 alone, more than 50 million people turned to food banks, food pantries, and community organizations for help.[51] Meanwhile, just over five percent of US households experienced a more severe form of food insecurity, regularly skipping meals or reducing their intake because they couldn't afford more food.[52]

There are little changes that you can make to help with that, from trying not to waste food to sharing excess food with neighbors. This can be particularly important in urban areas that are food deserts, where the only available options are gas stations and 7-11s. Sometimes, the only way for people to buy fresh produce is to drive for miles, and if they don't have a car, there isn't a bus that can take them.

Be willing to take part in and to create grass roots movements. For example, a half dozen people could get together to take it in turns to go to the store. Everyone could chip in ten dollars and each get a share of the fruit and veg.

Other organizations fighting food poverty include:

- Feeding America: www.feedingamerica.org
- No Kid Hungry: www.nokidhungry.org
- Meals On Wheels America: www.mealsonwheelsamerica.org

---

[51] "Hunger in America," *Feeding America*, accessed October 14, 2025, https://www.feedingamerica.org/hunger-in-america

[52] "Hunger & Poverty in America," *Food Research & Action Center*, September 10, 2024, https://frac.org/hunger-poverty-america

- Food Research and Action Center: www.frac.org
- World Central Kitchen: www.wck.org
- Feeding America's Hungry Children: www.feedingahc.org
- Blessings in a Backpack: www.blessingsinabackpack.org
- The Hunger Project: www.thp.org
- US Hunger: www.ushunger.org
- Why Hunger: www.whyhunger.org

This grassroots approach is how the San Francisco Bay cleanup started out–as a grassroots movement made up of local people who saw that something needed doing. It's the personification of that classic idea of being the change you want to see in the world.

On my walking route, there's a guy who follows the same route every day and takes a two-liter bottle of water with him. There are a few trees that weren't looking too healthy, and so he's been watering them along his way. He's been doing that for at least two years and now they're growing really nicely. Instead of looking dead, they're doing great.

It's a little thing, but there are over 8.2 billion people on the planet. If every one of us did something like that, it would make a huge difference.

Speaking of which, here are some organizations that specialize in cleaning up local neighborhoods:

- Keep America Beautiful: www.kab.org
- The Trust for Public Land: www.tpl.org
- American Rivers: www.americanrivers.org
- The Nature Conservancy: www.nature.org
- Groundwork USA: www.groundworkusa.org
- City Blossoms: www.cityblossoms.org
- Beautify Earth: www.beautifyearth.org
- Project for Public Spaces: www.pps.org
- Keep Houston Beautiful: www.houstonbeautiful.org
- Keep Atlanta Beautiful: www.keepatlantabeautiful.org

▷ **Action Item:** Choose one or more of the organizations on this list which resonate with you and browse their websites to find out more. If there's alignment between your own goals and those of the organization, consider reaching out to them and finding ways for the two of you to work more closely together.

One Last Story

Not too long ago, I had to pay a visit to the local police station, where I saw someone whose car had been towed. They were there to pay the fine, and they were clearly worried about how much it was going to cost them.

I was impressed by the woman behind the counter, who went out of her way to be kind, polite and caring to him. She knew he was going to suffer a significant financial hit, both because of the fine he'd had to pay to the cops and because of the charge he'd have to pay when he went to collect his car. She was so kind to him that despite the hardship he was facing, he was smiling as he walked away.

When it was my turn at the window, I went up and said, "Apart from what I need you to help me with, I wanted to let you know that I really appreciated the way that you dealt with the gentleman before me. It was a bad situation and it's going to cost him a lot of money, but you handled it with care and empathy and showed him that you cared about the fact that he was losing all of that money."

She told me that I'd made her day.

This, of course, is another great example of that virtuous cycle, because it meant that she went home feeling happy about her job and then at work the next day, she'd be in a good mood because of what I'd said to her. She'd be nice to someone else and the cycle would continue.

People are still going to have to pay their fines, of course, but at least they'll feel a little bit better about doing so because they'll be dealing with a person who doesn't think that just because they have to pay a fine, that means that they're a bad person or a criminal.

This story shows how you should never judge a book by its cover. I watched her as she listened patiently as he told her how he parked his car in the same place every day but always moved it before the time it was okay to park expired. Unfortunately, on that particular day, he got held up and didn't quite make it. He arrived just in time to see the car being towed away, but he was too late to do anything about it.

Of course, the woman at the counter could have told him to just shut up, pay the fine, and go away, but she didn't. Instead, she listened to his story with empathy and said, "Unfortunately, they're told that once they've hooked up the car, they can't leave it behind. That decision can't be reversed. I'm sorry it happened to you, but you know how it is. Rules are rules."

She wasn't in a position where she could change anything, but the way she dealt with the situation made the gentleman who was paying the fine feel better about the fact that he had to pay it.

CHAPTER TWELVE

Case Studies

"There comes a point where we need to stop just pulling out of the river. We need to go upstream and find out why they're falling in."

—Desmond Tutu

MY AIM WITH THIS chapter is to take a look at a few people who've inspired me throughout the years, especially if they've been able to successfully pivot from one area to another, or to dedicate a portion of their lives to public service.

I kicked things off with a quote by Desmond Tutu which encapsulates two things. The first is that age-old idea that prevention is better than the cure, because it's better to stop people falling into the river in the first place than it is to keep on dragging them out. The second is that it speaks to the need for us to help kids to get an education so that they can become self-sufficient, instead of waiting until they're adults and trying to help them out with welfare.

Tutu is the first person who's pivoted that we'll be covering in this chapter, but he may well be one of the most interesting. Born in 1931, he was a South African cleric who campaigned tirelessly against apartheid and was awarded the Nobel Peace Prize in 1984.[53]

Tutu provides us with some excellent examples of pivoting because he initially set out to start a career in medicine but was unable to afford the training. He became a schoolteacher instead,

---

[53] The Editors of Encyclopaedia Britannica, "Desmond Tutu," *Britannica*, October 3, 2025, https://www.britannica.com/biography/Desmond-Tutu

then attended Johannesburg's St. Peter's Theological College. In 1975, he became the first black South African to hold the position of dean of St. Mary's Cathedral.

By 1986, he'd been elected as the first black archbishop of Cape Town, and in 1995, South African president Nelson Mandela appointed him as head of the Truth and Reconciliation Commission, which aimed to uncover human rights abuses during apartheid. Even after his retirement, he continued to write and make occasional public appearances.

Not bad for a man who'd first set out to become a doctor.

Bill Gates

Born in Seattle in October 1955, Bill Gates is a computer programmer, entrepreneur, and philanthropist who's mostly known for being the co-founder of Microsoft. Gates displayed a passion for computing from an early age, writing his first piece of software at the age of 13 and founding a company called Traf-O-Data while still in high school.

As a sophomore at Harvard in 1975, Gates started working with Microsoft co-founder Paul Allen, eventually leaving the university during his junior year to create the company that would make his name—and his fortune.

In fact, Gates was a billionaire by 1986 and the richest person in the world from 1990 to 2010, with a peak wealth of over $100 billion.[54] But Gates is also a great example of someone who wanted his legacy to be about more than his financial success, which is why he recently dropped off Forbes' list of the ten richest

---

[54] Amelia, "Bill Gates Net Worth 2025: Salary, Age, Weight, Wife, Children, Awards and Investments," *Thornton's Budgens*, February 3, 2025, https://www. thorntonsbudgens.com/bill-gates-net-worth/#google_vignette

people in the world.[55] In fact, he's announced plans to donate 99 percent of his fortune to the Gates Foundation.[56]

And that brings me nicely on to Gates' pivot. Bill launched the Gates Foundation in 1994 with his then-wife Melinda, with the goal of funding global health programs. In 2006, fellow billionaire Warren Buffett came on board, donating around 40 percent of the foundation's overall funds.

As of 2025, the Gates Foundation aims to spend $200 billion on charitable projects over the next two decades, concentrating on goals like eradicating polio, reducing childhood malnutrition, and bringing malaria under control. They're an admirable set of goals, and a much better way to spend your money (and build a legacy) than on joyrides to space, at least if you ask me.

Florence Nightingale

Florence Nightingale was a British nurse and social reformer who's known today as being the mother of modern nursing.

Nightingale was well-educated and was able to read and write in French, German, Italian, Greek, and Latin from an early age. She showed little interest in the traditional "feminine" pursuits of the time, preferring to read philosophy and to engage in debates with her father.

When she was sixteen, she experienced a "call from God" in which she realized that her mission in life was to reduce human suffering. However, her family believed that nursing was an inappropriate activity for a woman of her intellect and breeding.

---

[55] Forbes Staff, "The top 10 richest people in the world (October 2025)," *Forbes Australia*, October 1, 2025, https://www.forbes.com.au/news/billionaires/the-top-10-richest-people-in-the-world-july-2025/
[56] Thalia Beaty, "Why Bill Gates is donating 99 per cent of his billion dollar fortune to Gates Foundation," *The Independent,* May 8, 2025, https://www.independent.co.uk/news/world/americas/bill-gates-fortune-foundation-wealth-b2747271.html

But Nightingale refused to conform to social norms and trained as a nurse in Germany before becoming the superintendent of the splendidly-named Institution for Sick Gentlewomen in Distressed Circumstances.

During the Crimean War, Nightingale led a party of 38 women to Barrack Hospital in Scutari, Albania, where she found conditions to be filthy and supplies to be inadequate. She ended up buying equipment with funds provided by the *Times* and talking soldiers' wives into helping with the laundry. By establishing standards of care throughout her wards, she was able to drastically reduce the mortality wait.

After the war, Nightingale established the first true nursing school, the Nightingale School of Nursing, at St. Thomas' Hospital in London in 1980. She was also the first woman to be awarded the Order of Merit, and International Nurses Day is celebrated every year on her birthday, May 12th.

When she died in 1910, Nightingale was so well-respected that she was offered a state funeral and burial in Westminster Abbey, but Nightingale had always been something of a reluctant hero and so her family turned it down. Instead, she was given a memorial service at St. Paul's Cathedral and then buried in the family plot in Hampshire.[57]

Nightingale's pivot from languages and philosophy to nursing is fascinating to me because she had to go against her family's wishes. She's a great example of how you sometimes have to make those kinds of sacrifices if you're to follow your passion and fulfill your full potential.

---

[57] Louise Selanders, "Florence Nightingale," *Encyclopedia Britannica*, September 30, 2025, https://www.britannica.com/biography/Florence-Nightingale

Greta Thunberg

Born in January 2003, Greta Thunberg was still a schoolgirl when she first made a name for herself as an environmental activist and campaigner for direct and swift action against climate change. [58] In 2018, she founded a movement called Fridays for Future, a youth-led and youth-organized movement that all began when Thunberg sat outside Swedish Parliament every school day, demanding urgent action. [59]

Thunberg's campaign picked up a huge amount of national and international press coverage, and she's continued to fight for climate action ever since. Today, she travels the world (avoiding planes because of their environmental impact), [60] meeting with global leaders and speaking at protests and other gatherings to demand action against climate change. She was nominated for the Nobel Peace Prize for five years in a row, from 2019 to 2023. [61]

Greta's story is interesting because when she pivoted, she was just a schoolgirl. She shows that you don't have to start out as a huge success or a superstar with millions of dollars in the bank to make a change in the world. You can start to make a change for the better before you even finish school—and these days, it's easier than ever before to do so thanks to social media.

Look at the number of people out there who've hit a million followers on their Instagram or TikTok before they leave school. That's also a reminder that your legacy doesn't have to be about

---

[58] The Editors of Encyclopaedia Britannica, "Greta Thunberg," *Encyclopedia Britannica*, October 8, 2025, https://www.britannica.com/biography/Greta-Thunberg

[59] Fridays For Future, "Fridays for Future – How Greta started a global movement," *Fridays for Future,* accessed October 15, 2025 https://fridaysforfuture.org/what-we-do/who-we-are/

[60] *"Fact Check: Does Greta Thunberg go out of her way to not use air p. . .,"* *Factually,* June 21, 2025, https://factually.co/fact-checks/environment/greta-thunberg-no-flying-rule-07d1a1

[61] Catherine Caruso, "Greta Thunberg," *Biography*, June 10, 2025, https://www.biography.com/activists/greta-thunberg

saving the world. It might just be that you're passionate about beauty or hair and makeup, and you want to teach people what you've learned—and if you're able to teach a million or ten million people, that's much better than having that passion but not sharing it with anyone.

People get very dismissive about social media influencers, especially when they're young. I think that's a shame. Whether they're a beauty influencer or a gaming creator, you can't put a price on the amount of joy they're bringing. If you're a beauty influencer and you help some kid who's always felt like an ugly duckling to suddenly feel like a swan, that's a huge accomplishment. You don't have to save the world; you can save one person at a time.

Wilbur Cross

Wilbur Cross was a Yale graduate who returned to earn a PhD in English literature in 1889, before being offered a job as a professor of English at Yale in 1894. He taught there for the next 36 years, becoming editor of the *Yale Review* and acting as Dean of the Yale Graduate School from 1916 to 1930.[62]

The Yale Graduate School has given out the Wilbur Cross Medal for Alumni Achievement every year since 1966 to honor alumni for outstanding achievements. Yale explains, "Medalists are nominated by their peers in recognition of their achievements as leaders in their respective fields, true innovators, and world-changing thinkers."[63]

When I was chair of the Graduate School Alumni Association, I got to read the citations for the nine medalists that were awarded during my two-year tenure, and that was quite a thrill because they were some pretty amazing people.

---

[62] "Wilbur Lucius Cross papers," *Archives at Yale*, accessed October 14, 2025, https://archives.yale.edu/repositories/12/resources/4034
[63] "Wilbur Cross Medal for Alumni Achievement," *Yale Graduate School of Arts and Sciences*, accessed October 14, 2025, https://gsas.yale.edu/about/awards-prizes/wilbur-cross-medal-alumni-achievement

Those nine people, by the way, were:

- Bernice A. Pescolido: sociologist and published author, as well as an inductee into the National Academy of Sciences.
- Fred Greenstein: political scientist whose work focused on political leadership and the US presidency.
- Huntington Willard: geneticist and head of the Marine Biological Laboratory, as well professor in human genetics at the University of Chicago.
- Jon Butler: award-winning historian and Howard R. Lamar Professor Emeritus of American Studies, History, and Religious Studies at Yale.
- Leslie Greengard: mathematician, physicist, computer scientist, and inventor, as well as co-creator of the fast multiple method algorithm.
- Paul Wender: the current Francis W. Bergstrom Professor of Chemistry at Stanford University.
- Stanley Fish: literary theorist, legal scholar, author, and intellectual.
- Stephen Greenblatt: literary historian and author who also won the Pulitzer Prize for General Nonfiction in 2012.
- Timothy J. Richmond: molecular biologist, biochemist and biophysicist.

Any one of those people could have been a case study in this chapter, and I'd encourage you to google them to find out more.

What's most interesting of all is that after Cross retired from the faculty and his deanship at the university, he chose to run for office. The site Connecticut History explains, "Serving as Connecticut's governor for two terms (1931-1939), Cross helped see Connecticut through the Great Depression, pushed for the repeal of Prohibition, and even presided over the opening ceremonies for the newly constructed Merritt Parkway in 1938."[64]

---

[64] "Wilbur Lucius Cross (1862-1948) | Connecticut History | A CTHumanities Project," *ConnecticutHistory*.org, accessed October 14, 2025, https://connecticuthistory.org/people/wilbur-cross/

Cross's pivot was particularly brilliant because he wasn't a natural politician. Remember, he was a professor and a dean, a lifelong academic, not the kind of person you'd expect to have great relationships with the populous at large. People normally think of professors and school administrators as having their heads in an ivory tower and only being able to communicate with other people who have the same level of education. The fact that Cross was able to transcend that shows that we're dealing with a person who didn't just pivot–he pivoted well.

Andrea Stella

Recently, I was in an art gallery in Florence where I discovered a painter named Andrea Stella.

Stella was born in Florence in 1950 and passed away in 2019. He started out as an apprentice, making frames for pictures and paintings. He was good at it, but he also knew that he didn't want to be a framer forever. Instead, he was fascinated by the works of art that he'd seen and wanted to create his own, and so he taught himself how to paint.

Stella's career change was a success, and he received a huge number of honors and awards throughout his career. His work has been exhibited at the Galleria degli Uffizi, the Palazzo Medici Raccardi, and the Hermitage Museum, and while his particular pivot didn't involve going into public service, it's still a great example of what you can achieve if you put your mind to it.[65]

Fauja Singh

Fauja Singh was a British marathon runner who provides us with an important reminder that it's never too late in your life to pivot. That's because he started running at the age of 89 as a way to

---

[65] "Biography," *Atelier Andrea Stella*, accessed October 15, 2025, https://www.atelierandreastella.com/about

overcome grief, and he continued to do so until he was well over 100, setting a bunch of age records along the way.[66]

We're talking about a guy who was born so long ago that the Guinness Book of Records refused to recognize him because he was born before the Indian government started keeping birth records.[67]

Most runners start in their twenties or thirties, but Fauja Singh isn't like most runners. He wasn't even able to walk until he was five years old, and his thin, weak legs meant that he struggled to cover long distances. His family had initially thought he was crippled.

Nicknamed the Turbaned Tornado, Singh achieved eight world age-group records in a single day in 2011, at the ripe old age of 100. Three days later, he became the first centenarian to complete a marathon.

Singh is a living example of that Maya Angelou quote, because when I started writing this chapter, I couldn't remember his name or the specifics of his achievements, but I could remember how his story had made me feel. That's part of his legacy. I never met the guy, but he still had a huge impact on my life—and, by extension, the lives of everyone who reads this book.

When I first wrote this section, Singh was still alive and well at 114 years old, although he'd finally hung up his running shoes and switched to attending events as a supporter. Tragically, he passed away during the editing stage, and not due to natural causes. He was killed in a hit-and-run while he was out walking.[68]

---

[66] Ronald Chettiar, "Fauja Singh: Oldest marathon runner an inspiration for youngsters," *Olympics.com,* July 15, 2025, https://www.olympics.com/en/news/who-is-fauja-singh-oldest-indian-origin-british-marathon-runner

[67] Adrian Goldberg, "100-year-old marathon runner not recognized by Guiness," *BBC News,* October 24, 2011, https://www.bbc.com/news/uk-15370205

[68] Saurabh Duggal, "Fauja Singh, world's 'oldest' marathon runner, dies at 114 in hit-and-run," *BBC News*, July 15, 2025 https://www.bbc.co.uk/news/articles/cpqnppnx0z1o

Very few people are fortunate enough to have a say in the manner of their death, but just like my mother-in-law, Singh wouldn't have wanted a long, drawn out death in a sickbed. It's somehow fitting that he died on his feet.

Leonardo da Vinci

I recently finished reading Walter Isaacson's biography of Leonardo da Vinci, who provides us with an interesting example of someone who didn't make a pivot because he didn't need to. Da Vinci was a man of so many talents that he essentially made pivoting his way of life. There's a reason why we think of him as the quintessential renaissance man.

You may have heard that da Vinci wrote backwards, which meant that his notes could only be read by looking at them in a mirror. Some people have said that he did this in an attempt to stop his enemies from being able to steal his work, but Isaacson offers a different explanation.

Leonardo da Vinci was left-handed, which meant that if he was writing from left to right, his hand was on top of what he was writing. If you're right-handed, you can see what you're writing as you're writing it. Da Vinci taught himself to write backwards because that way, he could see what he was writing. On top of that, it wasn't like he was writing with a Bic. Back then, when you wrote with a quill and ink, you'd smudge what you were writing if you wrote left-handed.

People have also speculated about why he wrote so much on every piece of paper, but there's a simple solution to that, too. Paper was expensive.

Interestingly, da Vinci's habit of reusing paper had the same inadvertent effect as his backwards writing, making it more difficult for other people to read his work. Unless you can age the ink on the page, it's difficult to tell whether something was written on the same day or whether he came back to that piece of paper ten years later.

The most amazing thing to me is that it's only because he wrote everything down that we can talk about what he did and try to decipher his work. We can read what he wrote and get the measure of him. I dare say that a hundred years from today, we're not going to be able to access any of our tweets and Facebook posts.

At the end of his book, Isaacson's call to action was to pick up a pen and paper so that somebody down the line can figure out who *you* are. That's kind of what I'm doing here, because a similar thought came to my mind. I have an 18-month-old grandson, and I thought that one day, when he's an adult and he wants to learn some more about his grandpa, it would be good for him to be able to pick up a book and read all about me.

Sure, he'll hear things along the way and hopefully have many years to get to know me before I pass, but you never know what the future will bring. Besides, people often don't realize they want to know more about people until it's past the point that they're around. If one of my grandfathers had written a book, I'd have been fascinated to read it, even though I talked to them a lot when I was a teenager. It's only now, with the power of hindsight, that I'd have a better appreciation of their lives and what they were thinking and feeling. And the fact that they've passed away means that a book would be my best option for having a "conversation" with them.

Besides, a book is also structured and carefully put together in a specific order. The author has had time to revise their words and to make sure that every sentence counts.

Going back to da Vinci, the fact that he wrote on paper means that we can read *everything*, even the stuff that he would have thought of as being a first draft. That's very different to what's happening here. Sure, my book might still exist in 500 years, but people won't be able to see all of the different drafts and the bits that were cut out and never made it. If I was doing this 500 years ago, that would still be lying around on sheets of paper, whereas today, it's all in my Dropbox file history.

Even if people could still access my Dropbox in 500 years, at some point in time, the file format will become obsolete. It's already happened to me within my lifetime. I used to record VHS videos of my kids when they were little, and I always meant to convert them to a digital format but never got around to it. A couple of years ago, I rediscovered a stack of tapes, but I had no way of viewing them. Fortunately, I found a local store that could convert them to a digital format for a small price. Now I have them all as MP4s, which is fine for now, but will they still work in 50 years? I doubt it.

My point here is that a lot of the stuff that we think is permanent is only temporary—and in fact, you could argue that there's no such thing as permanence. Still, our goal should be to build as permanent of a legacy as we're able to, whether that's so that we can look back and reflect on our lives, or whether it's so other people can learn about what we did and what we stood for. Your legacy is a measure of the person that you are, going further than just what people remember of you.

Shakespeare and Co.

I'd also like to touch upon people who've had words named after them, because in many ways, that's the greatest legacy of all. For example, when you hear the word "Orwellian," you immediately think of heavy surveillance and Big Brother watching you. That's an incredible legacy to have—it's not just that Orwell's works have stood the test of time. They've become so culturally significant that they've turned his name into a shorthand term for what his work stood for.

There are plenty more of them, too. For example:

- Darwinian: related to natural selection and survival of the fittest.
- Dickensian: characterized by poverty and social injustice or evocative of Victorian London.
- Freudian: relating to unconscious motives.
- Herculean: requiring great strength or effort.
- Kafkaesque: strange, twisted, and bizarre.
- Machiavellian: cunning, scheming and unscrupulous, especially in politics or business.
- Orwellian: characterized by oppressive government surveillance, propaganda, and totalitarianism.
- Shakespearean: grand, poetic or notably dramatic, especially when describing a tragedy.
- Sisyphean: used to describe a task that's pointless and never-ending.
- Victorian: of or related to the period of 19th century England during the reign of Queen Victoria.

The fascinating thing about these words is that whenever you use them, any native English speaker will immediately know what you're talking about. You don't need to go into any further detail. They can even conjure up mental images. Whenever someone says "Dickensian," I immediately picture the sooty streets of 19th-century London, filled with urchins and chimney sweeps. That just goes to show how powerful this form of legacy can be.

In Shakespeare's case, it's over 400 years since he died and we still have that association with his name. However, there are even examples of people who are still alive whose names are bywords, although I'm not convinced that they'll stand the test of time. Some examples that I uncovered during my research included Trumpian, Oprah-esque, Beyoncéan, and Rihannian.

It's also distinct from the other area where names are synonymous with things, which is brands and companies. You don't talk about picking up a facial tissue; you always reach for a Kleenex. You have a Hoover instead of a vacuum cleaner. Da Vinci needed a Bic, not a ball-point pen. And here are some others you might recognize:

- Band-Aid
- Dumpster
- Frisbee
- Jacuzzi
- Jet Ski
- Onesies
- Post-it
- Q-tip
- Thermos
- Tupperware
- Velcro
- Xerox

Brands want to build a legacy as much as people do. Most of them want to build a legacy based on money, but there are some notable exceptions including any of them in the non-profit sector, from Greenpeace to Butterflies and Amandla. If you're a non-profit and you haven't left a legacy behind, it's almost a sign that you haven't made as much of an impact as you could have or might have wanted to.

You can accidentally stumble into something that's going to leave a legacy behind, but it generally works a lot better when you're deliberate about it. Still, you might get your start because you accidentally fell into something and found that you had a passion for it, and that's just fine, too.

Just be careful not to fall into something that you're good at but which you don't have any passion for. That's a classic case of a time in which you need to pivot. Otherwise, you end up focusing on it until one day you wake up and say, "I'm not feeling fulfilled. I need to do something different. I can't keep doing this blindly for the rest of my life, just because I'm good at it."

Now, I'm not necessarily saying that you should give it up entirely, because that's not always feasible, especially when that's what's paying the bills. You might keep on doing it while doing something else on the evenings and weekends so that you can start to make a slow pivot and ultimately contribute more to the world.

At the end of the day, passion bleeds through.

Brandon Stanton

When I look at the people whose case studies we've featured, I'm struck by how every one of them was able to pivot or to carry out public service by putting their existing skills to good use.

You can follow in their footsteps by finding ways to apply your skills. Let's say that you're good at photography, but your real passion is to help underprivileged children. If that's the case, perhaps you could blend the two by going out to India and launching a project where you photograph the kids and tell their stories.

That reminds me of *Humans of New York*. The project was founded by Brandon Stanton, who explains, "I began Humans of New York in the summer of 2010 as a photography project. My initial aim was to take ten thousand photos of random New Yorkers and plot these photos on a map of the city. In the course of collecting these portraits, I naturally began having short conversations with the people I photographed. After several months, I began to experiment with adding small quotes to the portraits. Before long, these conversations became the focal point of the work itself."[69]

Since then, Stanton has released several books, the first of which instantly become a *New York Times* bestseller. In 2015, he became the first social media creator to photograph and interview a president in the Oval Office when he was invited to the White House by the Obama administration. And in the fifteen years since he first started out, he's raised over $20 million for the various people and causes he's featured both in New York and around the world.

---

[69] "Humans of New York," *Brandon Stanton,* accessed October 13, 2025, https://www.humansofnewyork.com/humans-of-new-york.

Funnily enough, someone took a photograph of me in Times Square a few months ago, and then he came up to me and showed me his camera. Unfortunately, I thought he was trying to sell me something and so I did the usual New York thing and just walked away. Perhaps he was just trying to ask me about my story.

I also had someone approach me in Notting Hill when I was in London. I'd just purchased a bowler hat in one of the used clothing stores and I was just standing there wearing it when someone came up to me and said, "I love your hat." Then he asked if he could take a photo of me.

I looked at him a little skeptically, but then he told me, "I'm an art student." He whipped out his portfolio, which he had a physical copy of, and told me that he was trying to make a book about people that he didn't know and that he'd first met when he'd asked them for their photograph. He had a little conversation with them, took their photo, and then included them in his book.

He actually had a whole bunch of paraphernalia set up, including lights and reflectors, so that he could take a proper portrait. Then he talked to me for a few minutes about who I was and what I did, and then six months or so later, he sent me a link to his university thesis, which included my photo and my story.

We tend to think of ourselves as the main characters in life, and we forget that every single person on this planet has a story of their own. That's why it's so important to work with kids like Amandla and Butterflies are doing. Everyone's got their own story to tell, but some of those kids would never get the chance to tell their story without what we're doing. They wouldn't get to live out their full stories.

A big part of my legacy comes from the fact that I've helped to empower people who might not otherwise have been able to achieve their full potential. They would have been brought down by poverty, disease, or the lack of an education. People get beaten down when they end up in those sorts of situations and they quit on themselves. Maybe they could have been a good painter, but they were too busy surviving to ever pick up a paintbrush.

We talked about how paper was expensive back in da Vinci's day. We should think of ourselves as fortunate that he was able to afford it. How many da Vincis were there that got forgotten by history or were overlooked?

Of course, their creative output isn't what makes a person's life valuable. It would be incredible if some of the kids in Amandla were to become great painters, writers, or philosophers, and it's important to give them the opportunity if that's what motivates them, but at the same time, they don't have to go off and achieve something like that to have lived a valuable life.

There's a lot to be said about helping people to fulfill their basic needs by providing them food, water, shelter, and safety. As long as you're doing that, you've done a great thing. If they go off and become amazing at something, that's incredible. If they go off and live a "normal" life, that's equally incredible. And you'll have done something amazing just by taking some of their suffering away.

At the end of the day, what could be a better legacy than that of giving people the opportunity to live without undue stress and suffering just to stay alive?

A Life of Meaning and Impact

"All we have to decide is what to do with the time that is given us."

–Gandalf to Frodo in *The Fellowship of the Ring* by
J. R. R. Tolkien[70]

WHEN I FIRST LEARNED about science and scientists, I thought that if I wanted to become one, I'd have to be just like the stereotypes in terms of being super introverted and not having many friends or talking to too many people. I thought I'd just go off and do my work.

That continued throughout my school and college years, but every once in a while, I'd find myself enjoying the company of people who did things other than science. It never occurred to me that I was missing out on a part of life and failing to embrace my extroversion.

It wasn't until I went to Yale that I found myself as a human being. I ended up staying in a graduate dorm where I had a tuba player from the school of music on one side and someone who was studying economics on the other. That opened my mind up to a whole bunch of possibilities.

I realized I needed to look outside my sphere of expertise, and so that's how I started seeing the world in the way I do now. It's also the reason why I went into applied physics instead of pure science, specializing in plasma physics with a little bit of electrical engineering.

---

[70] J.R.R. Tolkien, *The Fellowship of the Ring* (United Kingdom: George Allen & Unwin, 1954).

When I first arrived at Yale, I went to the university commons, which is a dining area with huge oak-paneled walls. I noticed that the walls were inscribed with the names of a bunch of people, but I had no idea who they were or why their names were up there. I'm naturally curious and don't like not knowing things, and so I asked one of the faculty members about it. He told me that he'd have to get back to me because he didn't know.

A couple of days later, the faculty member got back to me and said, "These are people who were awarded the Yale Medal, which is given to people in recognition of their lifelong or transformational volunteer service for Yale after they graduated."

I didn't think anything of it at the time. I had no idea that my name would one day join them.

In 2020, I was awarded the Yale Medal for my service to Yale, and now my name is up on that wall, too.[71]

Why Not?

When I look back over the six plus decades of my life, I come to the conclusion that a lot of the times I've made a pivot in my life, it's because when I asked the question "why," I also asked, "Why not?" I'd encourage you to do the same throughout your life.

In fact, I suspect that anyone who does so will learn more from the "why not" than they will from the "why." After all, it's easy to get comfortable and to find yourself saying, "Why should I change my life? I'm happy and I'm comfortable. That's good enough for me."

Change always brings uncertainty with it, but I find that asking "why not?" helps to open up the possibility that you're going to be doing something new and exciting, something that will fulfill and enrich you in ways that you've never imagined. It can set you

---

[71] "They deserve a medal," *Yale Alumni Magazine*, https://yalealumnimagazine. org/articles/5209-they-deserve-a-medal

free and provide you with the little prod that you need to make the switch from slavishly doing what you were doing yesterday to following your passion and doing something different today.

In *The Matrix Resurrections*, there's a scene where one of the characters is explaining that every human being is stuck in a quandary between wanting more than they've got and being afraid of losing what they have. In the movie, that's what keeps people stuck in the matrix. And in reality, it's what stops people from pursuing a more fulfilling life and experiencing their full potential.

The reality is that nothing comes without risk. Every entrepreneur who starts a business is taking a huge risk by doing so, but the payoffs can be enormous. There are plenty of examples of people taking risks and getting rewarded for doing so, and we've covered quite a few of them in this book.

Unfortunately, we often see the opposite happen, too. Just look at the movie industry, which keeps pumping out sequels, prequels, and reboots of its favorite franchises. Movie execs keep milking the same formula because they can predict the results and it's an easier way of making money than taking a risk on something new.

And taking risks doesn't always work out. Look at all of the musicians who quit their bands to go solo, their solo attempt failed, and they ended up having to get back together with their former band.

Then there are corporations and the products they make. Often, they're afraid to set aside what they've done and to try something new. Apple is one of the few companies that seems willing to discontinue products when they've reached the end of their natural lifespan. They do that even when a product is selling like hot cakes because they know they've got something better but that no one will give it a chance unless you take away the old stuff. That's just what being human means. We don't like to leap into the unknown.

It's just like that quote we had earlier that's falsely attributed to Henry Ford, where he said that if he'd asked people what they wanted, they would have said faster horses. At the time, they didn't know what a car was. They would have thought of it as a horseless carriage.

> ▷ **Action Item:** Revisit the action item from chapter one, where I asked you to say yes to something that you'd normally say no to. This time, if your instinctive reaction is to say no to something, focus on the "why?" and "why not?" Either think of a reason why not to do it or try it.

Baby Steps and Coin Tosses

In a lot of ways, it's difficult to reach beyond what you know. That's true in many different areas of life, from work to relationships. We get stuck because we don't want to experience uncertainty, but we forget that uncertainty is an opportunity, rather than a threat. Yes, change for the sake of change isn't good, but if change comes about organically as a byproduct of you following your heart, it's generally positive.

When you face a situation where you have to make a change, it forces you to examine the situation you're in, and a little self-reflection goes a long way because it helps you to figure out what is and isn't working. It also helps to show you why making a change might be a good thing.

The minute you start to analyze this stuff, you get the courage to take the next step, which should be a baby step. Don't just say, "Oh, I'm fed up with my career, I'm going to go off and do this new thing, and I don't need to worry about anything else." That's rarely the right thing to do. Instead, you should dip your toe into the water.

Try doing something new a bit at a time, keeping your primary employment while you do a little moonlighting. If it doesn't work out, at least you tried something different and figured out that it's not for you.

Perhaps you're thinking about changing from one industry to another, or maybe you've pivoted from working for profit to working for a non-profit organization. You might have switched from enriching your own life and the lives of your family to helping other people to do the same. Perhaps you've started working to create a better environment for future generations. Whatever the case, the same principle applies. You have to start by asking the questions "why?" and "why not?"

If it helps, you can list out your whys and your why nots and see which side has the most arguments. You may find that there are more arguments for one side or the other, but sometimes the side with the fewest arguments is also the side with the strongest ones. Sometimes you look at the arguments against doing something but realize that you still want to do it, kind of like when you flip a coin to make a decision, see what the coin lands on and realize you want to overrule the coin.

Deep down, you probably know the answer to your "why?" or "why not?" but sitting down and structuring your thoughts like this can make it easier for you to take action. Tossing a coin can help, but coin tosses are random. Listing out the whys and why nots is like a coin toss on steroids. You get the same effect in terms of it clarifying your thoughts and making you feel that disappointment if the wrong answer comes up, but it can also help you to articulate the reasoning behind that disappointment.

Going back to Maslow's Hierarchy of Needs, it's a lot easier to take a risk if you're only risking the top of the pyramid. Besides, self-actualization and esteem are inherent to doing something you love and that you're good at. You'll naturally lose some of that esteem if you try and fail, but it's better to risk and lose something like that than to risk your shelter and access to food and water and lose that.

And so my call to action here is for you to take a look at where you are on that hierarchy. It doesn't mean that you can't take a risk if you're towards the bottom of it, living paycheck to paycheck, but it does mean that if you find yourself in that situation, you need to be a little more careful. That's a great example of a time when it's best to try moonlighting and to take those baby steps. If you've got all of that stuff covered, you can afford to take bigger risks; instead of dipping your toe into the water, you can dip your whole foot in. But you're still not going to want to dive on in!

The idea of dipping your toe into the water is a cliché, but it's a cliché for a reason. If you dip your toe into the water and you find that the temperature is okay, you can dive right in. And if you dip your toe into the water and it's too hot for you, you can find a way to add more metaphorical cold water. Ask yourself, "How am I going to modify the inputs so that I can try again?"

If you look at what I did with the Yale Graduate School Alumni Association, I started dipping my toe in the water by agreeing to temporarily join the board. There, I found that the water was fine and so I stayed on, but in another universe, perhaps I might have found that the water was too hot. If that had happened, I might have worked with recruitment or given some talks to the students without sitting on the board.

The same is true for Amandla and Butterflies. When I was asked to do the voiceover for Butterflies, I might have tried it and decided that I wasn't comfortable doing that but that I still wanted to help.

Ultimately, my point here is that you need to keep trying until you find something that works for you. If you dip your toe into enough baths, eventually you'll find one that's the perfect temperature.

> ▷ **Action Item:** Find some baths to dip your toes into. Keep up the search until you find a Goldilocks bath that's "just right."

PIP = ML

We've all heard of Einstein's famous formula, $e=mc^2$, although not everyone understands what it means. For the record, it can be broken down as energy = matter multiplied by the speed of light squared. Robert Lamb and Yara Simón explain, "[The formula] asserts that mass and energy are interchangeable. In practical terms, this means that a small amount of mass can be converted into a vast amount of energy and vice versa. Einstein's equation opened the door for numerous technological advances, from nuclear power and nuclear medicine to understanding the inner workings of the sun."[72]

I'd like to draw this book to a close with a formula of my own: PIP=ML. Don't worry, though—my formula is a lot easier for you to wrap your head around than Einstein's. It goes a little something like this:

$$\text{Passion + Purpose + Impact = Meaning + Legacy}$$

Essentially, if you're fortunate enough to be passionate about something and to find your purpose in that passion, the next step is to put that passion and purpose to work and to make an impact out there in the real world. It's only by putting those three puzzle pieces together that you'll be able to find meaning in your life and ultimately to build a legacy.

When passion, purpose and impact align, people are willing to undergo extraordinary hardships as they build their legacy. They're willing to take punches and even bullets to change society, because they know that they're doing something not for themselves but for the people who come after them. When an activist endures batons and bullets, they do it not because they themselves will benefit from it but because they understand that

---

[72] Robert Lamb and Yara Simón, "E = mc2: What Does Einstein's Famous Equation Really Mean?," *HowStuffWorks*, September 19, 2023, https://science.howstuffworks.com/science-vs-myth/everyday-myths/einstein-formula.htm

they're doing what they're doing to make the world a better place so that other people won't have to suffer as they did.

In my case, my passion is helping people, and my purpose is to reduce the suffering of children as much as possible. I've been able to make an impact through my work with Butterflies and Amandla, and that's helped me to find meaning in my life and ultimately to build my legacy.

Now it's time for you to start building yours.

Your Impact Shift
Turn Passion into Purpose

Dr. Prasad's work is guided by a simple principle: **Passion + Purpose + Impact = Meaning + Legacy (PIP = ML)**. Moving toward impact doesn't require a grand gesture—just one intentional step.

Option 1: Financial Impact

Support Dr. Prasad's philanthropic work with marginalized youth through education and community initiatives in India and South Africa. Contributions through U.S. boards such as **Butterflies** and **Amandla** go largely to the children and communities they serve.

Take action: **Visit the organizations below to make a contribution.**

Your Impact Shift
Turn Passion into Purpose

Option 2: Time & Talent Impact

Offer a practical skill—writing, design, translation, social media, or research—to support a board or similar organization. Even a small, one-time contribution can make a meaningful difference.

Take action: Reach out through the organization's contact form and offer your expertise for a specific task.

Your Impact Shift
Turn Passion into Purpose

Start converting your passion into purpose right in your local community. Remember, it doesn't have to be a major commitment, it just has to align with what excites you.

Your Reflection: What small, conscious step will you commit to taking today to begin your Impact Shift? Write it down:

I will commit to:

Every challenge is an opportunity, and every first step is a courageous leap of faith.

Acknowledgments

I RECENTLY WALKED alongside the Zimbabwe side of the Victoria Falls, where there's always a huge spray of mist due to the water flowing over a 355-foot drop.[73] As it was a clear day, the sun was shining and I saw a number of vivid rainbows, each of which seemed to start at my feet. A thought occurred to me.

The pot of gold at the end of the rainbow isn't far away from us, at the other end of the rainbow. It's buried right at our feet. We rarely see the riches we have now because we're too busy searching for riches elsewhere.

As for me, I'm well aware of the riches I have, and they come in the form of the people who share their love, kindness, and support with me. Allow me a few paragraphs to acknowledge and thank them for everything they've done for me.

First of all, this book wouldn't exist without my wife, Sharmila. I've known her for 46 years, and she's been my friend since the beginning, my best friend for 45 years and my wife for 41. She's the one person who's constantly pushed, cajoled, and encouraged me to be the best possible version of myself, and she's always given me the latitude to go off and do things when other people might have said, "Hey, wait, that's stupid."

Next up, we have my elementary school teacher, Geeta Dudeja, who always used to tell us to aim for the stars. All of these years later, I'm still doing exactly that.

Thanks go to Steve Scher, who looked at my response to a survey from the Yale Graduate School Alumni Association (GSAA) and

[73] "Victoria Falls National Park," National Parks, accessed October 13, 2025, https://national-parks.org/zimbabwe/victoria-falls.

chose me to fill a vacant seat on the board. It was the start of a lifetime of volunteer service on behalf of and in service to Yale University.

To Julia Downs of the Yale Alumni Association, who took me under her wing as I joined the GSAA Board and showed me all that I could do as a volunteer through constant encouragement and gentle pushes in the right direction.

To Jenny Chavira, Deputy Executive Director of the Yale Alumni Association, whose friendship and guidance helped me to navigate the world of alumni relations and taught me so much about being a volunteer in an organization that also has paid staff.

To Weili Cheng, who started as the Executive Director of the Yale Alumni Association the same time I became chair, for teaching me that there's life after retirement (she joined Yale after retiring as a lawyer and chief legal counsel of Ritz Carlton Hotels) and becoming a lifelong friend. And we're on the same path again, as she's enjoying spending time with her first grandson, who's six months older than mine!

To my dear friend Joe Gerardi, who asked me to help translate the video material he'd received from Butterflies in India and then chose me to narrate the video even though I had no prior experience.

To Scott Clark, Founder and Executive Director of Amandla for infecting me with his passion to help take the youth of Philippi from cradle to college. He has been such an inspiration and a great partner to work with.

To my dear friend Pulin Sanghvi, who has grown to become a brother to me, for the hours of long walks and conversations on all manner of topics that helped inform my thinking about my career pivot.

To the folks at Leaders Press, particularly Alinka Rutkowska and Andrew Dupy for believing in my story and Chona Marie Tan for reaching out to me through LinkedIn and asking provocative questions about why I should *not* write my story.

I owe a huge a debt of gratitude to all of these people and to so many more. I wish I had the space to list you all, but alas…

And last, but by no means least, I thank you, dear reader, for taking the time to read this book. I hope that you've found it inspiring and useful.

About the Author

Dr. Rahul R. Prasad is a distinguished physicist, philanthropist, and bestselling author whose career spans academia, advanced research, and humanitarian service. Born in New Delhi, India, Dr. Prasad moved to the United States in 1982 to pursue graduate studies at Yale University, where he earned an MS, MPhil, and PhD in Engineering and Applied Science after completing a BSc (Hons) in Physics from St. Stephen's College, University of Delhi.

Dr. Prasad began his professional journey as a research scientist in the Department of Mechanical Engineering at Yale University (1986-1989), conducting pioneering work on understanding turbulence in fluid flows. He went on to hold several key research positions in California, including physicist III at Physics International in San Leandro (1989-1991), senior physicist at Science Research Laboratory in Alameda (1991-1994), and principal scientist at Alameda Applied Sciences Inc. (1994-2001). From 2001 to 2018, he served as senior physicist and manager at the Lawrence Livermore National Laboratory, contributing to national research and technological innovation in the area of nuclear fusion.

In 2019, Dr. Prasad transitioned from scientific research to focus on philanthropy and global development. He currently serves as president of Butterflies USA in New York, supporting marginalized youth in India, and as chairman of Amandla Development Inc., an organization empowering youth in South Africa through education and community initiatives. Additionally, he is a limited partner at MVP Ventures in Menlo Park, California, where he advises on scientific and technological ventures.

An active Yale alumnus since 2002, Dr. Prasad has served in several leadership roles, including chair of the Yale Graduate School Alumni Association (2010-2012), chair of the Yale Alumni

Association Board of Governors (2016-2018), and currently as a member of the executive committee of the Yale Alumni Fund Board of Directors. His service reflects his deep commitment to higher education and mentorship.

Beyond his professional and philanthropic achievements, Dr. Prasad is also a USA national bestselling author of *Success DNA: Mastering Persistence in Leadership and Life*, featuring his chapter "The Many Facets of Success." His writing explores the intersection of leadership, resilience, and lifelong learning—core values that define both his personal and professional journey.

Dr. Prasad is an avid photographer, traveler, and adventurer who has explored all seven continents, capturing remarkable wildlife and landscapes. His photographs have been exhibited in local galleries and recognized with awards. He is also a student of history, particularly American history, and values meeting new people and learning from their experiences.

He lives in California with his wife, Sharmila, and their two dogs, Hamilton and Mason—named after Founding Fathers Alexander Hamilton and George Mason. He has two children, a son-in-law, and a grandson. Guided by his belief that "the day you stop learning is the day you are six feet underground," Dr. Prasad strives to leave the world better than he found it through knowledge, compassion, and purpose.

Websites:
rahulrprasad.com
butterfliesusa.org
amandladevelopment.org
500px.com/rrprasad